KU-769-493

150 SCANDINAVIAN KNITTING DESIGNS

Mary Jane Mucklestone

Search Press

A QUARTO BOOK

Published in 2013 by Search Press Ltd
Wellwood
North Farm Road
Tunbridge Wells
Kent TN2 3DR

Reprinted 2014

Copyright © 2013 Quarto Publishing plc

All rights reserved. No part of this publication
may be reproduced, stored in a retrieval system
or transmitted in any form or by any means,
electronic, mechanical, photocopying, recording
or otherwise, without the permission of the
copyright holder.

ISBN 978-1-84448-934-3

Conceived, designed and produced by
Quarto Publishing plc
The Old Brewery
6 Blundell Street
London N7 9BH

QUAR.KDS

Project editor: Victoria Lyle
Art editor and designer: Julie Francis
Illustrator: Luise Roberts
Photographer (swatches): Phil Wilkins
Photographer (projects): Simon Pask
Proofreader: Caroline West
Indexer: Helen Snaith
Art director: Caroline Guest
Creative director: Moira Clinch
Publisher: Paul Carslake

Colour separation in Hong Kong by Modern Age
Repro House Ltd
Manufactured in China by 1010 Printing
International Ltd

CONTENTS

FOREWORD

I grew up greatly influenced by Scandinavian textiles. My great-grandma was Norwegian and, although no one in my family knitted, we wore Scandinavian sweaters and there was lots of other needlework in our home. My hometown of Seattle has a large Scandinavian population and their influence was pervasive. At school my classes were full of peers wearing classic Scandinavian knitwear: lots of versions of the Norwegian Lusekofte, brightly coloured Greenlanders, Fana Sweaters with stars and undyed Icelandic Lopapeysas. Additionally, I spent many hours in Seattle's great shops, which feature cutting-edge modern Scandinavian design, as well as the Nordic Heritage Museum, which celebrates both old and new design. While knitting the swatches for this book I found many elements familiar from my childhood within the patterns.

Though the subject 'Scandinavia' is ridiculously large to squeeze into one book, I've attempted to give you a nice cross section of pattern designs, some very old and some decidedly contemporary, for Scandinavian design is always evolving. I hope you'll use this work as a jumping-off point for your own Scandinavian textile designs and discoveries.

Mary Jane Mucklestone

ABOUT THIS BOOK

This book is a knitter's directory of over 150 Scandinavian designs, each one designed to inspire. The style of the charts is easy to read and the layout of the book means that, whether you are looking for a combination of designs or just one to use as the focal point of a garment, you will find numerous possibilities here.

ESSENTIAL SKILLS

This section explores the essential skills you will need to knit Scandinavian designs. Including circular knitting, stranding, steeking and applying designs to projects, it will demystify the techniques involved and give you the confidence to start right away.

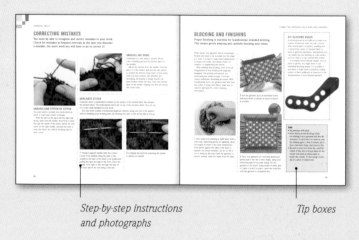

Step-by-step instructions and photographs

Tip boxes

Written instructions

List of materials

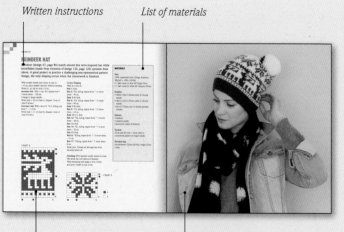

Colour charts

Styled photograph

PROJECTS

The designs in this book can be combined and used in a myriad of ways. This chapter presents a selection of stunning projects, with full making instructions, to inspire you with ideas of how to use the motifs.

DESIGN SELECTOR

This colourful visual selector displays all the designs side by side. Flip through for inspiration and to choose your design, then turn to the relevant page to create your chosen design.

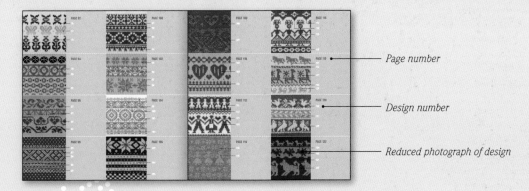

Page number

Design number

Reduced photograph of design

DESIGN DIRECTORY

The directory includes a stunning, actual-size photograph, a black-and-white chart, a colour chart and a colour-variation chart for each of the 100 designs.

Design number, row and stitch count

Black-and-white chart

Colour chart

Colour-variation chart

Mix-and-match chart

Actual-size photograph of design

ESSENTIAL SKILLS

This section explores the essential skills you will need to knit Scandinavian designs. Including circular knitting, stranding, steeking and applying designs to projects, it will demystify the techniques involved and give you the confidence to start right away.

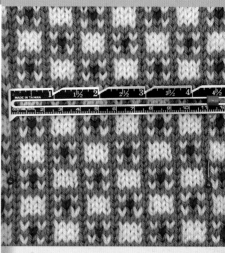

YARN

Scandinavian colourwork knitting can be worked in just about any yarn, but it is instructive to take a look at the wool used in traditional garments of the region.

The original landrace sheep of Scandinavia were descendants of the North European short-tail sheep. Landrace are domesticated wild sheep that naturally adapted to their environment. By natural selection and rudimentary breeding, distinct local varieties of sheep developed, such as Gute, Finnsheep and Speslau. There are regional differences in flocks, even of the same type of sheep, as fleece is determined not only by the animal's genetic makeup but also by its diet and environment.

All of these small, sturdy, primitive breeds have dual coats, consisting of a coarse hairy outer coat and a fine downy undercoat, in an array of natural colours. Different yarns were made by separating the two coats and making studied choices when spinning. The natural sheep colours were blended for a wide range of colours and complemented with local natural dyestuffs as well as dyes procured from trading, such as indigo for blue and madder for red.

Though most commercial Scandinavian wool today comes from improved breeds, modern yarns retain some characteristics of the original wools, being sleek, glossy, light and resilient. These yarns are perfect for stranded knitting. The natural crimp helps the floats stay in place, and assists in holding a garment together when steeks are cut. The worsted-spun wools give great stitch definition for clear patterning. Working at different tensions can produce diverse results, from a tight, woven-like surface to a loose knit with a luxurious drape.

TRADITIONAL SCANDINAVIAN YARNS

It is not within the scope of this book to present all of the many yarns produced in the region, but it is worth mentioning a couple of especially interesting ones.

FINNISH LANDRACE OR FINNSHEEP

A lovely, soft wool containing a lot of lanolin, making it especially warm. Riihivilla, a family run Finnish business, lovingly selects fleeces that are then minimally processed and spun to high standards. They offer seven natural shades as well as a range of 100% naturally dyed colours. The yarns are available in two weights: Aarni, a 4-ply; and Maahinen, a fingering weight. This gorgeous yarn has a slight halo when knit up, and is excellent for fulling and felting, so take care when washing!

ICELANDIC WOOL

Icelandic sheep were brought to the island by Viking settlers 1,100–1,200 years ago and have remained fairly unchanged since that time. Their fleece is dual coated: the long outer coat – called 'tog' – is glossy and water-repellent, while the inner coat – called 'thel' – is fine, soft and highly insulating. The two coats are processed together to create a lofty, warm, and strong yarn.

Icelandic handknitting yarn is lightly spun and comes in four weights: Einband, lace weight; Létt lopi, DK or 4-ply; Álafoss lopi, Aran weight; and Bulky lopi, chunky weight. Additionally, Plötulopi is a single-ply, unspun yarn sold in flat rounds called a 'plate'. Though fragile to use, once knit up its long fibres create a sturdy yet very soft garment. Should the wool pull apart while knitting it is easy to spit-splice it back together.

OTHER YARNS

Any type of yarn can be used to knit Scandinavian designs. Just be aware of their individual properties and the effects these will have on your designs.

SUPERWASH

Superwash yarns are highly processed, allowing them to be machine washed and even machine dried. This processing also makes the wool less scratchy, meaning many are able to wear garments right next to the skin. Superwash yarns are a bit 'slippery', which would seem to make them a less-than-ideal choice for garments requiring steeking. However, that is not the case – it is just these qualities that make superwash wools a very popular choice for Scandinavian knitting – just take special care to reinforce steeks, preferably by using a sewing machine.

MOHAIR

Mohair is made from the hair of the Angora goat. The exceptionally long fibres make a yarn that is durable and resilient with a high sheen. Stranding with mohair will soften the outlines of any pattern, as the long fibres make a long, thick halo over the surface. Though often seen as a drawback in patterned knitting it can be used to great effect, producing a unique garment. The fibre does not felt like wool does, so machine steeking is recommended.

ANGORA

Angora is made from the downy coat of the Angora rabbit. The famous Bohus knitting co-operative of Sweden went to great lengths to develop exceptional angora-blend yarns. The wonderful fluffiness of the fibre diffuses the patterns, blurring the edges. Angora has very little memory and so may best be used as an accent or highlight. Some people have difficulty knitting with angora since the 'fur flies'. If you are sensitive, look for a blend with a low percentage of angora to wool. Keep in mind that angora is very insulating and as a result may be very, very warm – a little bit of angora can go a long way!

COTTON, LINEN AND OTHER PLANT FIBRES

Cotton was used in traditional Scandinavian knitting, sometimes stranded with a wool yarn. When using plant fibres, be aware that the yarns are often heavy and stranding will make your garment weighty. Since the floats do not mat at all, wrapping the floats every few stitches is recommended. Plant fibres are inelastic with very little memory, and tend to grow lengthways during the wearing. Washing and blocking will bring them back to their original size, only to grow again between washings! Let these qualities work to your advantage therefore by planning designs that factor in the fibre's inherent qualities.

ALPACA

Yarn from alpaca, bred for thousands of years in South America, can be a great choice. It is a supple and soft fibre that is heavier than wool. Since alpaca contains no lanolin, those sensitive to sheep wool often find they can wear it. The fibres are hollow, making them very insulating and warm. The fibres have less memory than wool, with a tendency to drape. Be mindful of this when making tension swatches; let them hang vertically for a while so you get an idea of how much the piece may grow lengthways. However, consider it an asset, giving your garment an elegant swish. Alpaca comes in a range of natural browns and the white takes dye brilliantly.

NOVELTY YARNS

There is a wide variety of novelty yarns; try them out for modern, new looks. What may not work for a garment – for example, some fun fur – may be sensational in a simple, graphic pattern on an afghan. A glitzy, metallic yarn might liven up a traditional pattern, bringing some modernity to an otherwise old-fashioned garment. Be bold, be brave, like much of modern Scandinavian design!

BALL BAND INFORMATION

Ball bands will give you varying amounts of information about your yarn.

- Company logo (1)
- Yarn name (2)
- Length of yarn in the ball (3)
- Weight of yarn in the ball (4)
- Recommended needle size (5)
- Colour (6)
- Dye lot (7)
- Care instructions (8)

Finnsheep

Icelandic

Superwash

Mohair

Angora

Linen

Alpaca

NEEDLES AND OTHER EQUIPMENT

There is a whole array of materials and equipment at your disposal, from essentials such as a tape measure and scissors, which you will probably already have in your sewing or knitting kit, to useful gadgets to make your life easier. This section provides an overview of what is available.

Needle gauge

KNITTING NEEDLES

Knitting needles are an investment because you will use them time and time again. Look after your needles carefully and they will last for years – but when the points are damaged or the needles are bent, it is time to throw them out and buy new ones. Since most Scandinavian knitting is done in the round, you will be using circular needles and double-pointed needles of various sizes and lengths.

CIRCULAR NEEDLES

Circular needles allow you to work in the round, using plain, or knit, stitches, to create a seamless fabric. The weight of the knitted piece rests on your lap, so this type of needle is useful if you are working with a heavy or chunky yarn.

They consist of two rigid tips of metal, plastic, wood or bamboo, joined by a length of plastic or nylon cord. The material your needles are made from is purely a matter of personal choice, but it is essential to get needles that have a smooth join between the cord and the needle.

Like straight needles, circular needles come in a range of sizes (diameters) to suit different weights of yarn. The size depends on what kind of yarn you are using and on your own personal tension. If you are following a pattern, your tension must match that of the pattern.

Circular needles are also available in different lengths, from 30–150cm (12–60in) or more. The length of the needle you use depends on the number of stitches needed for the item you are knitting: 60–80-cm (24–32in) lengths are customary for sweaters, 40-cm (16in) lengths for sleeve tops and hats. However, the needle length must be shorter than the circumference of your work.

DOUBLE-POINTED NEEDLES

If the circumference of the piece you are knitting is smaller than 40cm (16in), double-pointed needles are used. Double-pointed needles are customarily used for small items such as mittens, gloves, socks and the crowns of hats. Double-pointed needles come in sets of four or five. Like circular needles, they allow you to work in the round and change direction. This is useful when turning the heel on a sock, for example. They were traditionally made of steel, but aluminium, bamboo and plastic are more common now.

OTHER EQUIPMENT

Although all you really need are needles and yarn, a few extra accessories will help to make your projects go much smoother. Choose beautiful gadgets that you will treasure for years.

NEEDLE GAUGE

Not all needles are marked with a size and the small ones look frustratingly similar. A needle gauge is really handy for checking the size of unidentified needles. It has a series of holes to indicate size: just push the needle through the holes until you find the one nearest to its diameter.

STITCH MARKERS

Stitch markers come in a variety of styles and you will want to try them all. Bright plastic rings close in size to that of your needle are very helpful for marking off stitch repeats. Use a different colour to indicate the beginning of the round. Locking stitch markers are useful for making vertical notations, such as counting rounds. They are also useful to mark the beginning of the round when using double-pointed needles, where ring markers would slide off.

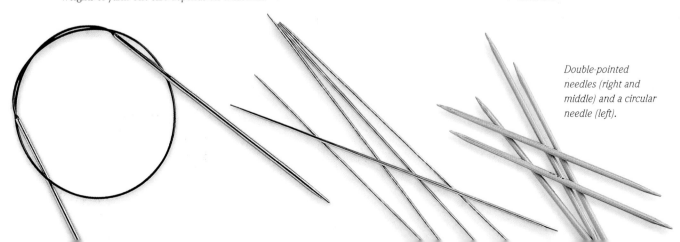

Double-pointed needles (right and middle) and a circular needle (left).

Stitch markers

Scissors

Tape measure

Tapestry needles

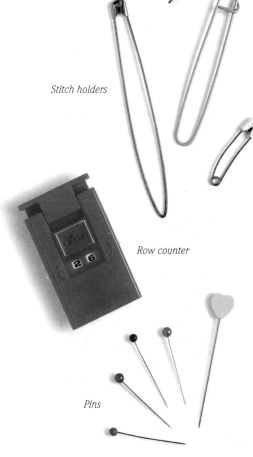

Stitch holders

Row counter

Pins

Pom-pom makers

SCISSORS
Small, sharp scissors should be used to cut yarn. Never try to break yarn with your fingers – some yarns are very strong and will cut your skin.

TAPE MEASURE
The best tape measures for knitters are the retractable dressmaking type. It is best to have one marked with both centimetres and inches.

TAPESTRY NEEDLE
For weaving in ends and grafting stitches, you need a blunt-tipped needle with a large eye (like a tapestry needle). These are available in a range of sizes to suit different yarn types.

STITCH HOLDERS
These devices work like large safety pins and are useful for holding the stitches at the bottom of a steek or at the tops of shoulders, for instance.

ROW COUNTER
A row counter is helpful for keeping track of rows or rounds, provided you remember to click it! The barrel type is fitted onto a straight needle; for large-sized straight needles or for circular knitting, you need the clutch type.

PINS
Large-headed pins are the best type to use when measuring your tension or pinning garments in place while blocking, because the large coloured heads won't get lost between the stitches.

PENCIL, NOTEBOOK, TAPE
Pencils are handy for making notations on patterns, ticking off rows and jotting down adjustments. A notebook is nice for making a note of new ideas and inspirations. Little ones with graph paper are especially useful for making up your own Scandinavian designs. You could tape snips of yarn from your colourways next to the chart, corresponding to their order of use.

BLOCKING AIDS
Although neither of these are things that you would normally associate with knitting, they are useful to have around: balloons are great for blocking hats, while dinner plates between 23–28cm (9–11in) in diameter can be used for blocking tams.

POM-POM MAKER
Fantastic for fashioning perfectly spherical pom-poms.

HELPFUL FOR KEEPING YOUR PLACE ON THE CHART
Post-it notes, a magnetic ruler and/or a clear plastic ruler can be moved along a chart as you work, making it easy to keep track of exactly where you are in the pattern.

13

TENSION

Before you start a knitting project, it is absolutely essential that you knit a swatch to measure your personal tension. The tension of a piece of knitting is the number of stitches and rows (or rounds) counted over a given measurement – usually a 10-cm (4in) square.

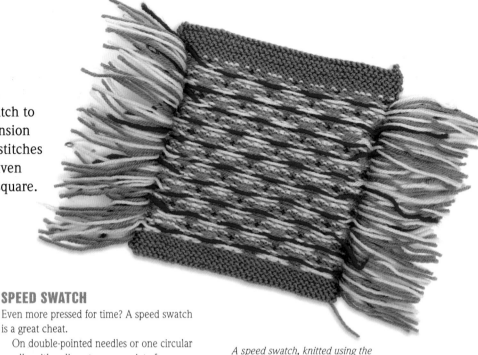

A speed swatch, knitted using the same stitch pattern as the planned project, showing broken yarns at each end.

Whether you are following a written pattern or designing your own, you will need to know your tension – in the first case to make sure that the garment will come out to the desired size and in the second case to calculate the number of stitches and rounds you need for your design.

Scandinavian tension swatches should be knit in the round. Ideally, this means casting on enough stitches to be able to knit comfortably on a 40-cm (16in) circular needle. The number of stitches you need to cast on will vary depending on the yarn used – a rough guide is to multiply the desired stitch tension per centimetre of the pattern you are following by the length of your circular needles in centimetres. Knitting a swatch of this size will allow you to measure 10cm (4in) of your work without having to cut it to measure it. Work rounds in the Scandinavian pattern until the swatch measures about 13cm (5in) long, then cast off or place your stitches on a piece of scrap yarn.

If you don't want to devote that much time or yarn to making a tension swatch, use fewer stitches and double-pointed needles. You will need to cut your swatch so that you can measure it flat, so this is also a good opportunity to practise steeking.

TIP
Begin with a ribbed or garter stitch border to help prevent curling.

SPEED SWATCH

Even more pressed for time? A speed swatch is a great cheat.

On double-pointed needles or one circular needle with a diameter appropriate for your yarn, cast on enough stitches for a generous-sized swatch – ideally, the projected number of stitches for 13cm (5in). If you are following a written pattern, cast on the number of stitches the tension calls for, plus 2.5cm (1in) worth of stitches.

Using the same stitch pattern as in your project, knit across. When you reach the end of the row, break both yarns and slide the work back to the right-hand end of the needle. Join in the yarn again, and knit across as before. In this way, you will be creating only knit stitches, just as you would if knitting circularly.

Continue knitting in this manner until you have a square about 13cm (5in) in size, then cast off.

ALTERNATE METHOD
Instead of breaking the yarns, leave very, very long floats that span the swatch from behind. You will then cut the floats, so you can measure the swatch accurately.

CREATING A FABRIC TO SUIT YOUR NEEDS

Altering the size of the needles you use will affect the type of fabric you create: the fewer the number of stitches and rounds to the centimetre, the looser the fabric. Conversely, the more stitches and rounds to the centimetre, the tighter the knitted fabric will be. If you are designing your own project, make swatches using different sizes of needles to help you decide which fabric best suits your needs.

MEASURING YOUR SWATCH

When you've completed your swatch, wash it and block it (see page 29). When it is dry, place it on a hard surface, and measure it as shown (below). If you find that you have more rows or stitches than the pattern suggests, the tension is too tight and you should change to a larger needle. If there are fewer stitches or rows, change to a smaller needle.

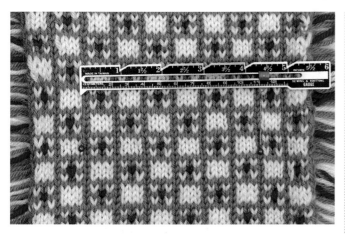

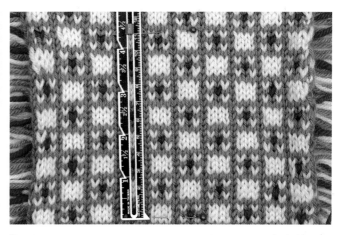

1 Using a ruler or a tape measure, place two pins exactly 10cm (4in) apart at the centre of the swatch, as shown. Count the number of stitches along a straight row between the pins.

2 Now place the pins 10cm (4in) apart vertically and count the number of rows between them, along a straight line of stitches.

Swatch 1 was made using DK yarn and size 5 (3.75mm) needles. It has a tension of 5 stitches and 5 rounds to the centimetre, making a relaxed fabric with large stitches and visible spaces between them. This might be a nice fabric for a throw.

Swatch 2 was made using DK yarn and size 4 (3.5mm) needles. It has a tension of 6 stitches and 6 rounds to the centimetre. This is a standard tension for sweaters; the stitches are even, with no spaces between them. The resulting fabric is flexible, yet firm.

Swatch 3 was made using DK yarn and size 3 (3.25mm) needles. It has a tension of 7 stitches and 7 rounds to the centimetre. This is a good tension for mittens and gloves, creating a dense fabric with very small stitches.

CASTING ON

To begin knitting, you need to cast on some stitches. Here are four of the most versatile ways to cast on.

The cast-on method you choose depends on the outcome you require – an elastic or firm cast-on, decorative or plain. Different methods of casting on give different results, suitable for different purposes. Sometimes, an extra-strong cast-on may be required – for example, on children's garments where edges may be prone to hard wear. For other garments, a cast-on that has more stretch may be needed. Try them out to see and feel the difference. In all cases, the tail ends can be used for sewing up seams or woven in unobtrusively (see page 23).

All the methods shown here begin by making a slip knot, which serves as the first stitch.

TIPS

• To ensure that your cast-on stitches are not too tight, use a needle one size larger than called for.

• A more delicate cable cast-on is made by taking the needle into the newest stitch each time, instead of between the stitches. This creates a useful edge for hems.

MAKING A SLIP KNOT

Putting a slip knot on the needle makes the first stitch.

Loop the yarn in the direction shown, leaving a tail of desired length (see tips box, left). Use the needle tip to catch the yarn inside the loop. Tighten the knot gently in the needle.

BACKWARD LOOP CAST-ON

Not recommended for the foundation of a garment, this cast-on is perfect for adding stitches at the end of a row or over a buttonhole opening.

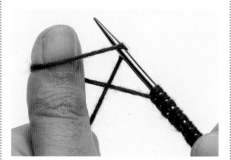

Leaving a short end, make a slip knot on the needle. Tension the yarn in your left hand and make a loop around your thumb. Insert the needle into the loop, slip your thumb out and pull the yarn to make a stitch on the needle.

CABLE CAST-ON

This cast-on is made by knitting a stitch, then transferring it from the right needle back to the left needle. It is a firm cast-on that makes a strong edge with a ropelike twist.

1 Put a slip knot on one needle. Holding this needle in your left hand, insert the other needle into the front of the slip knot. Take the working yarn around the right-hand needle and pull through a stitch, then transfer it to the left-hand needle.

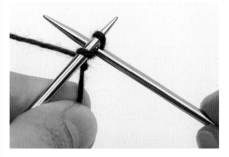

2 Insert the right-hand needle between the new stitch and the next stitch and make another stitch as before. Continue in this way for the desired number of stitches.

LONG-TAIL, OR CONTINENTAL, CAST-ON

This method creates a firm foundation row that mimics a row of knit stitches. Although it seems tricky at first, requiring nimble fingers, it is the fastest cast-on once mastered. Begin by measuring off about three times the length of the edge to be cast on. Make a slip knot and place it on the needle. Keep the yarn coming from the ball at the back and the shorter tail end in the front of the work.

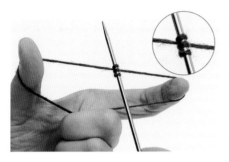 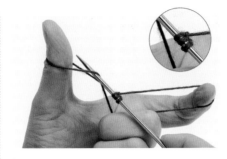

1 Hold the needle in your right hand and both ends of the yarn in your left hand. Wrap the tail around your left thumb from back to front and loop the other strand around your left index finger. Grasp both strands in the palm of your hand with your remaining fingers.

TIP
Measuring out three times the length of the cast-on edge can be challenging. To work out how much yarn you will need, cast on 10 stitches and then unravel them. By measuring the unraveled yarn, you can calculate how much yarn you will need. An alternate method is to use two balls of yarn. Join both ends on the needle with a slip knot, then cast on using both balls. Cast on one extra stitch. Break off one ball, and undo the slip knot.

2 Slide the needle up through the loop on your thumb.

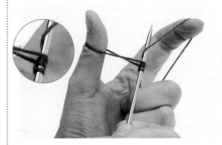

3 Take the needle over the top of the yarn on your index finger and draw this through the thumb loop.

4 Release the thumb loop and pull to tighten it around the needle. Repeat until you have the required number of stitches.

THUMB CAST-ON

This method achieves the same edge as the long-tail cast-on.

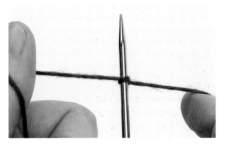

1 Measure off about three times the length of the edge to be cast on and make a slip knot on the needle. Hold the needle and yarn from the ball in your right hand.

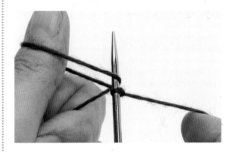

2 Tensioning the other end of the yarn in your left hand, make a loop around your thumb and insert the right needle into the loop.

3 Take the yarn around the needle, then draw a loop through to make a stitch. Gently pull the end to close the stitch up to the needle. Repeat until the required number of stitches, including the slip knot, have been cast on.

CIRCULAR KNITTING

Circular knitting, or knitting 'in the round', creates a tubular fabric with no seams. Traditional Scandinavian garments are almost always knitted in the round, because by knitting circularly, the right side always faces you, allowing you to see your work and watch the progression of your pattern.

WORKING WITH CIRCULAR NEEDLES

Knitting in the round is worked on a circular needle for the body of garments.

With circular needles, the needle length should be 5cm (2in) or more shorter than the circumference of the piece to be knitted: a circular needle will accommodate stitches equivalent to approximately twice its length. A circular needle that is too long for the number of stitches will stretch the knitting, and the stitches will not easily slip around it, making the knitting process difficult.

TIP
To make a smooth cast-on edge, without a little step where the first round begins, cast on one more stitch than required. Arrange the circular needle or double-pointed needles ready to work the first round and then slip the first stitch from the left needle onto the right needle. Lift the next stitch on the right needle over the slipped stitch.

1 Cast on the required number of stitches. Lay the needle on a flat surface, with the tips away from you and the tip with the working yarn on the right. Arrange the stitches evenly around the needle, with the cast-on edge to the inside all round. Make sure that the cast-on edge is not twisted around the needle, or the knitting will be twisted, too.

2 Pick up the needle, lifting the needle tips toward you. The tip with the working yarn should be on the right. The yarn itself should lie loosely outside the circle, not down through the centre.

3 To mark the beginning/end of the round, slip a ring marker onto the right needle tip. Knit the stitches as required. Every few stitches, push more stitches to be worked up the left needle tip, and spread out and slide the new stitches away from the right needle tip, so that all the stitches slip around the flexible cord. When you reach the marker again, one round is complete. Slip the marker and begin the next round.

WORKING WITH FOUR DOUBLE-POINTED NEEDLES

Knitting in the round is worked on double-pointed needles when the stitches are too few to fit on a circular needle – when knitting sleeves, the tops of hats, socks or other small projects, for example.

Double-pointed needles should be long enough to hold one-third of the required stitches (to work on four needles) or one-quarter (to work on five needles). If the needles are too short, the stitches will tend to drop off the tips.

1 Cast the required number of stitches onto one long, ordinary knitting needle. Slip one-third of the stitches purlwise onto one of the double-pointed needles.

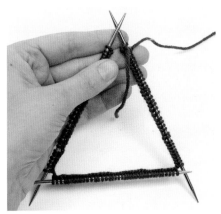

2 Slip the remaining two-thirds of the stitches onto two more double-pointed needles. Some patterns stipulate an exact number of stitches on each needle; otherwise just divide the number of stitches into three. Arrange the needles in a triangle, so that the working yarn is at top right. The cast-on edge should be inside the triangle. Push each group of stitches toward the centre of each needle. The leading tip of each needle should overlap the next needle.

3 Pick up the work, bringing the needle tips with the working yarn towards you. The working yarn should be outside the triangle, not down through the centre. Use the fourth needle to knit all the stitches on the first needle. Arrange the new stitches together at the centre of the fourth needle. The first needle is now empty: use it to work the stitches on the second needle, and so on.

WORKING WITH FIVE DOUBLE-POINTED NEEDLES

Sometimes it is more convenient to work on a set of five needles. In this case, divide the stitches evenly between four of the needles and use the fifth needle to begin the round.

4 Work the first and last stitches on each needle quite tightly, keeping the needles close together to prevent gaps caused by loose stitches. To mark the beginning/end of the round, place a ring marker one stitch from the end of the last needle – that is, one stitch from the end of the round (otherwise it will fall off). Slip the ring marker on every round.

TIP
When using double-pointed needles, arrange the stitches so that entire pattern repeats are on each needle; this will make it easier to 'read' your work.

HOLDING THE YARN

In traditional Scandinavian colourwork knitting, there are never more than two colours in any row, so you only have two yarns to control at a time. Experiment to find a method that you feel comfortable with.

There are several different ways of holding the yarn in Scandinavian colourwork knitting; three are shown, right. Try them all to find out which works best for you. Though they may feel funny at first, remember, you learned to knit with one strand of yarn, so you can learn to knit with two or three or more yarns, it just takes practice. Keep the tips of your fingers as close to the needles as you can to make working the stitches and controlling the tension easier.

You will want to hold your pattern colour in the most dominant position (see yarn dominance, page 21), which is usually the strand farthest to the left, in whichever method you are using. However, the most important thing is to be consistent with the position of both yarns throughout the piece.

ONE YARN IN EACH HAND
Hold the background colour (red) in your right hand and the pattern colour (grey) tensioned between the fingers of the left hand. Knit the background yarn by moving it into place with your right index finger, and the pattern yarn by picking it up with the tip of the right needle, pulling it forward through the loop, and off the needle.

BOTH YARNS IN RIGHT HAND, OVER INDEX AND MIDDLE FINGERS
Hold both yarns in the right hand, with the background colour (red) over the index finger and the pattern colour (grey) tensioned over the middle finger. Knit the background colour by manipulating the index finger; for pattern stitches, turn the hand slightly to flick the yarn from the middle finger around the needle.

BOTH YARNS IN LEFT HAND, OVER INDEX FINGER
Wrap both yarns around your index finger from front to back, with the pattern colour (grey) to the left of the background colour (red). To knit, insert the right needle into the next stitch and, with the tip, select the yarn required, pulling forwards through the loop, and off the needle.

THREE OR MORE YARNS
When using three or more yarns, use a combination of left- and right-handed techniques. It may be slow going at first, but with practice you will become adept.

TIP
Try practising on a project with just two colours and a simple design with a repeat of eight stitches or fewer, until the stranding becomes easy for you.

STRANDING

In this type of knitting, the colour not in use is carried loosely across the wrong side of the work. The loose strands formed are called 'floats'. For a neat appearance on the right side of the work, one colour float should always lie 'below' and the other colour float 'above', all across each row. Simple stranding is effective for pattern designs with fewer than nine stitches between colour changes, as the floats are not long. Longer floats can be tamed by using the weaving technique (see pages 22–23).

SIMPLE STRANDING

1 To change from the pattern yarn to the background yarn, simply begin knitting with the background yarn, stranding it above the pattern yarn, and knit the required number of stitches. Keep the previous pattern stitches spread out along the right needle so that the the strand of background yarn behind the stitches is not too tight.

2 To change from the background yarn to the pattern yarn, begin knitting with the pattern yarn, stranding it below the background yarn, and knit the required number of stitches.

On the reverse of the fabric the floats or yarn strands should lie parallel and should not be twisted around each other. For an even appearance, it is important that the floats of each yarn lie consistently either under or over the other. The grey pattern float lies under the red background float.

MANAGING FLOATS

While stranding, make sure that the floats do not become too short, as this will cause a puckered fabric. As you knit, take care to smooth your work out along the right-hand needle. In this way, the yarn not in use will strand along behind the just-knitted stitches, and will automatically be the correct length. With practice, smoothing out your just-knitted stitches will become second nature. Floats that are too long are less of a problem, but they can make the stitches too tall, making your work look uneven.

YARN DOMINANCE

In stranded knitting, one yarn will appear slightly more dominant than the other. Yarn dominance occurs because one yarn's strand travels slightly farther than the other, making it slightly tighter, causing it to recede, and be less dominant. The yarn travelling the shortest distance is the dominant yarn. Another way of putting it is that the yarn that comes from below will dominate, while the yarn from above makes a slightly smaller stitch.

Usually the pattern yarn is held to the left of the background yarn, making the pattern colour dominant, but there are slight differences in individual technique.

The most important thing is to be consistent in holding your yarn. Assign one position to the pattern colour and one to the background colour; always keep them in the same position while knitting your piece.

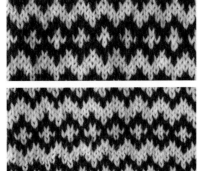

On the top swatch, the grey stitches are larger; on the bottom swatch, the white stitches are larger.

When we look at the wrong side, on the top swatch the grey strands are beneath the cream strands and on the bottom the cream strands are beneath the grey strands.

WEAVING

Some Scandinavian colourwork designs have many stitches between colour changes. Where a colour passes behind more than eight stitches, it should be woven over and under one or more of those stitches to prevent long, loose floats that can catch on fingers and jewellery.

Weaving is used when the yarn not in use has to be carried across the back of the work for more than eight stitches. There are also other instances when you might care to weave in floats: Some yarns, such as superwash baby yarn, do not have the same 'sticky' properties as traditional, minimally processed 100% Scandinavian wool yarns. Thicker yarns make larger stitches, therefore longer floats, which you may want to tack down. A good rule of thumb is not to allow a float to be longer than 2.5cm (1in). Weaving is also a good option for some children's items such as mittens, so little fingers will be less likely to be caught up in a long float.

Weaving in makes a denser and therefore less flexible fabric than simple stranding; if you weave every stitch, the resulting fabric will almost mimic a woven fabric. Consider your project: this could be an asset for a mitten which needs to be hard wearing, but not what you would want for a flexible cozy cowl.

Sometimes the woven float shows through on the right side of the garment; this is most noticeable with highly contrasting colours. When you need to weave, take care to stagger where you catch the floats. If you catch one right above another, you may inadvertently create a vertical line.

WEAVING WITH BOTH HANDS

WEAVING BACKGROUND YARN
1 Work to the point where the background yarn needs to be caught.

2 Lay the background yarn across the pattern yarn.

3 Insert the needle through the next stitch, over the background yarn, catching the pattern yarn, and pulling it through the loop and off the needle.

4 Bring the background yarn back to its original position.

WEAVING PATTERN YARN
Work to the point where the pattern yarn needs to be caught. Insert the needle into the next stitch, and under the pattern yarn, wrapping the background yarn as usual, pulling through the loop and off the needle. Continue knitting the background colour as usual.

WEAVING WITH THE LEFT HAND

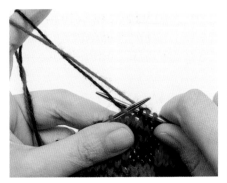

WEAVING BACKGROUND YARN
Work to the point where the background yarn needs to be caught. Insert the right needle into the next stitch; use the left thumb to bring the background colour forward. Bring the right needle tip behind the pattern yarn, from right to left, and scoop it forward, through the loop, and off the needle. Release the background yarn on your thumb and resume knitting as usual.

WEAVING PATTERN YARN
Work to the point where the pattern yarn needs to be caught. Insert the right needle into the next stitch and, with the tip, reach under the pattern yarn to catch the background yarn from right to left, and pull it through the stitch and off the needle. Resume knitting as usual.

WEAVING WITH THE RIGHT HAND

WEAVING BACKGROUND YARN
Work to the point where the background yarn needs to be caught. Drape the background yarn across the pattern colour. Knit the pattern colour. Move the background colour back to the original position.

WEAVING PATTERN YARN
Work to the point where the pattern yarn needs to be caught. Lay the pattern yarn across the background yarn, and knit the background yarn. Move the pattern yarn back to the original position.

WEAVING IN ENDS

Weaving in the loose ends may seem tedious, but it is a task that needs to be done. One approach is to weave in the ends of the old yarn while joining in the new yarn. Leave a tail of yarn about 15cm (6in) long when you join in the new yarn, then thread the yarn end onto a tapestry needle and run it along the back of a row, up and down through about ten stitch loops. After completion, pull gently to tighten the yarn, then snip off any excess.

Try to weave them back into the same row in the direction they are coming from. You may weave them into the purl 'bumps' on the back of the work, or hide them beneath small floats, or you might choose to be more exacting and follow the course of the stitches.

You might consider eliminating ends altogether by spit-splicing old and new colours together.

Weave in ends by catching the purl bumps along the same round of knitting.

Weave in ends by embedding the yarn under small floats.

INCREASING AND DECREASING

Although traditional Scandinavian garments are made with very little increasing or decreasing (and most increases or decreases will not show very much, because of the complexity of the two-colour surface), these are basic knitting skills that you need to master.

INCREASING

Many traditional Scandinavian garments have a blocky shape, with increases usually made only on the edges of garments, at the beginning of a round, at the halfway point or 'seam line' or just before or just after steek stitches.

To place them in the middle of a row/round upsets the pattern motif, requiring a total redesign of all subsequent patterning, and is only done on intricately designed pieces. Increasing in the middle of rows/rounds can be done on plain rounds of only one colour. Keep in mind, increasing in this manner will affect pattern motif placement on subsequent rounds, so design your garments accordingly.

Increases are also used when knitting sleeves from the cuff up, where stitches are increased on either side of a centre underarm 'seam stitch'. Increases can also be decorative, as in the gusset shaping on the thumb of mittens or gloves.

There are many ways to increase and most knitters have their own favourite method. Patterns do not always specify how to increase and may just give the instructions to 'make' a number of stitches.

Here are three increase methods that work well.

KNITTING INTO THE BACK OF THE BAR BETWEEN STITCHES
This increase is worked in between two stitches.

1 Work to where the extra stitch is needed. Pick up the bar created by the yarn between the stitches by putting the right needle through it from back to front and place on the left needle by inserting it under the strand from front to back.

2 Knit through the back of this loop as if it were a stitch and slip it from the left needle.

KNITTING INTO THE STITCH ONE ROW BELOW
This is worked by picking up and knitting into a stitch one row below.

1 Work to where the extra stitch is needed. Put the right needle through the top right side of the knitted stitch one row below.

2 Place this stitch on the left needle without twisting and knit it as normal.

KNITTING INTO THE FRONT AND THEN THE BACK OF A STITCH
This increase is worked either at the beginning or end of the knitted piece, as it is not particularly neat. Use it on the edge or one stitch in from the edge, so that it will be lost when the pieces are sewn together.

1 Work to where the extra stitch is needed. Knit into the front of the next stitch on the left knitting needle without slipping it off.

2 With the stitch still on the left needle and the yarn at the back, knit into the back of the stitch and slip it from the needle.

DECREASING

Decreasing is done to shape necklines, sleeve openings and sleeves. It is important to know how the stitches will lie with different decreases and increases. For example, when losing stitches around a neck detail, it is preferable that the stitches lie in the direction of the decrease: in other words, stitches on the right side of the neck need to form a slope that points to the right, while stitches on the left side need to form a slope that points to the left. That said, Scandinavian knitters often go against this convention and work the decreases pointing away from the decrease in order to have the colour of their choice on top.

As Scandinavian knitting is generally done in the round, with the right side always facing, all the methods shown below are on right-side rows.

RIGHT-SLANTING DECREASE (K2TOG)
Knitting two or more stitches together on the right side of the work creates a slope to the right.

1 Put the knitting needle knitwise through the second and then the first stitches on the left needle.

2 Knit the two stitches together and slide both from the left needle.

LEFT-SLANTING DECREASE (SSK)
This stitch slopes to the left and creates a mirror image of the k2tog decrease.

1 Slip the first stitch knitwise. Slip the second stitch knitwise. (They must be slipped one at a time.)

2 Insert the left needle tip through the front loops of both slipped stitches together. Wrap the yarn around the right needle tip, as shown.

3 Lift the two slipped stitches over the yarn and off the needle, leaving one new stitch on the right needle.

TIP
If you'd like something more than just a blocky-shaped garment, try changing the size of your needles: go down a needle size or two to shape waists. Another idea is to shape by decreasing or increasing evenly around in the plain rows between pattern designs. The only drawback with this method is that the pattern designs may not line up vertically.

WHAT COLOUR TO USE?

Work both increases and decreases in whatever colour will keep your pattern correct. For instance, in the chart right there is a one-stitch increase on round 4: use the pattern colour so that it looks as if the increase stitch is part of the next pattern repeat. In round 8, on the decrease stitch, use the background colour, otherwise there would be a superfluous pattern stitch.

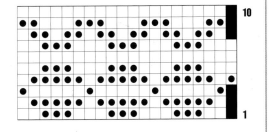

STEEKING

Steeking is a technique that enables you to continue knitting in the round without interruptions for openings such as sleeve holes or necklines.

Circular knitting creates seamless tubes, which can form the basis of many garments – scarves, mittens, gloves, hats, socks, skirts and bags, to name but a few. The bodies of sweaters and cardigans, however, need openings for necklines, sleeves and front openings.

Steeks are extra stitches used to bridge the gap where an opening is needed, allowing you to continue knitting in the round. When the knitting is complete, these extra stitches are cut down the centre with sharp scissors, creating an opening where sleeves may be attached or a neckline or button band picked up.

Steeks can be as tiny as three extra stitches or as generous as 12; between six and ten is usual. When knitting steeks, the principal rule is to use every colour featured in the round, creating a dense fabric with very short floats.

It is helpful to keep the stitch closest to the body of your garment in the background colour, making a 'fold line'. Use an even number of stitches for steeks, keeping the centre two stitches in the same colour, making it clear where to cut.

If you are using a traditional, minimally processed, 100% Scandinavian wool, which grips to itself, it is possible to cut the steek opening without special finishing, as stitches are reluctant to unravel laterally. If you are fearful or are using a less forgiving yarn, try either of the following finishing methods.

MACHINE- OR HAND-SEWN STEEK

This method is highly recommended for use with all 'slippery yarns', such as superwash yarns, mixed-blend yarns or yarns made from plant fibres or synthetics. It is also useful for large-diameter yarns, which may not stick together as readily as finer yarns do. The machine stitching ensures the yarns are locked into place.

1 Using a sewing machine, sew a line of stitches down the centre of the two columns of stitches that abut the two centre stitches. If you don't have a sewing machine, you can hand sew your steek with regular sewing thread, using backstitch. I recommend sewing it twice to really nail down the stitches. Work the second line of machine stitching one stitch over from the first line of machine stitching.

2 Carefully snip between the centre stitching lines. You may find it easier to snip from the wrong side, as the sewn stitches will be easier to see, making it less likely that you will accidentally cut through them: they will not be buried in the valley of a knit stitch. Pick up the stitches toward the body of the garment to add a button band or neckline. Then turn the cut edges to the wrong side just beyond the machine-stitched lines and tack in place if desired.

Sew down the centre of the two columns of stitches that abut the centre stitches (yellow). Cut between the centre stitches (white).

CROCHETED STEEK

Although it is time-consuming to do, the crocheted steek creates a lovely finished edge.
Use a crochet hook slightly smaller than the diameter of the knitting needles used.

1 Turn your work so that the left side of the opening is nearest to you. You will be working a line of double crochet by connecting the outside half of one of the two centre stitches to the neighbouring half of the stitch next to it.

2 Pick up the loops of the closest centre stitch (the one at the bottom of the steek) and the one immediately below it on your hook.

3 Wrap the yarn around the hook, then pull the hook through the two loops on the hook. Repeat to form the first double crochet stitch.

4 Continue, picking up the pairs of stitches immediately to the left. When you reach the top of the steek, cut the yarn and finish off. Turn the work 180 degrees, so the right-hand side of the steek is nearest you. Repeat steps 1 through 4 until you reach the end of the steek, then fasten off.

5 Carefully cut down the centre of the steek, between the two centre stitches. The cut edges will naturally roll to the wrong side along the crocheted stitches, making a tidy finish. Tack in place if desired. Pick up the stitches towards the body of the garment to add a button band or neckline.

Crochet the outside half of one of the centre stitches to the neighbouring half of the stitch next to it (yellow). Cut between the centre stitches (white).

CORRECTING MISTAKES

You must be able to recognise and correct mistakes in your work.
Check for mistakes at frequent intervals as the later you discover
a mistake, the more work you will have to do to correct it!

UNRAVELLING STITCH BY STITCH

You may need to unravel your work stitch by
stitch to reach and correct a mistake.

With the yarn at the back and the right side
facing, insert the left needle, from front to back,
through the centre of the stitch, below the next
stitch on the right needle, and pull the yarn to
undo the stitch. You will be working back in
each colour.

UNRAVELLING ROWS

Sometimes you will need to unravel whole
rows of knitting and put the stitches back on
the needles.

Slip all the stitches from the needle, hold the
piece on a flat surface, and pull the yarn gently
to unravel the stitches. Keep track of how many
rows you have undone, and whether any
increasing, decreasing or design feature has
been worked within the area. Place the stitches
back on the needle, making sure they are facing
the correct way.

DUPLICATE STITCH

Duplicate stitch is embroidery worked on the surface of the knitted fabric that imitates
the knitted stitch. The embroidered stitch sits on top of the incorrect stitch. You can use
it to cover small mistakes in your work.

You may work a series of horizontal duplicate stitches, along one row of the pattern
without breaking your working yarn, by weaving the yarn on the wrong side as you go.

1 Thread a tapestry needle with the correct
colour. From behind, bring the yarn to the
outside at the base of the stitch to be duplicated,
pulling the yarn through to the front. Place the
needle, from right to left, through the base of
the stitch above the one being corrected.

2 Complete the stitch by returning the needle
to where you started.

BLOCKING AND FINISHING

Proper finishing is essential for Scandinavian stranded knitting. This means gently washing and carefully blocking your items.

When damp, your garment will be surprisingly flexible and ready to be moulded into the shape you want. It is easy to make minor adjustments in length and width, narrowing a waist, for instance, or lengthening the sleeves.

With washing and blocking, most, if not all, irregularities in your knitting will magically disappear. The knitting will smooth out, eliminating any surface bumps. If you are using a traditional, minimally processed 100% Scandinavian wool, the garment itself will relax and soften. If using other fibres, make sure to read the ball band for correct washing information.

2 Roll the garment up in an absorbent towel and press down to extract as much moisture as possible.

1 First, wash your knitting in tepid water with a mild soap, squeezing gently, not agitating. Rinse thoroughly in water of the same temperature. Press gently against the sides of the basin to squeeze out excess moisture, but do not lift it out or wring as this may cause the garment to stretch; instead, drain the water from the basin.

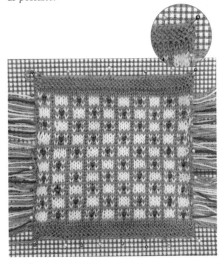

3 Place your garment on a blocking board and gently push it into the correct shape, using your measuring tape for accurate sizing. Pin the garment to the board, using rustproof safety pins or T-pins to hold it in place. Leave the board flat until the garment is completely dry.

DIY BLOCKING BOARD

A blocking board is not difficult to make; just a piece of plywood, with one side covered with several layers of quilters' wadding and covered with a piece of checked fabric to assist in garment placement. Alternatively you can simply lay your knitting on a flat surface, such as a bed or a rug covered with towels.

For smaller, more intricate shapes, such as socks or gloves, you might wish to use individual blocking shapes. It is possible to buy these or make them yourself by cutting a piece of thick cardboard or foamcore to the measurements of your finished garment.

TIPS
- Be generous with pins!
- After drying on the blocking board, the ribbing of your garment will also be stretched. If you'd like it to draw in, wet the ribbing again so that it relaxes, pin it into a narrower shape, and leave to dry.
- Be sure to store your knits flat, carefully folded. If they are to be put away for the winter, fold them in tissue paper to lessen the creases. To discourage moths, slip in a piece of cedarwood.

USING COLOUR

Traditional Scandinavian stranded knitting often uses just two colours.
However, even two colours can create a great variety of effects.

TRADITIONAL COLOURS

Traditional Scandinavian stranded
knitting often uses just two colours
from a limited palette such as black
and white, grey and white, red and
green, or a combination of natural
sheep colours. Just these colours
can create striking and varied
designs. However, I love colour and
believe knitting is a living tradition;
therefore many other palettes are
used throughout the book and I
encourage you to experiment,
bearing a few pointers in mind.

Reindeer in traditional colours.

Reindeer in modern colours.

VALUE

The first and most important
consideration when choosing
colours for your knitting is value,
the lightness or darkness of a
colour. For the most crisp and
clear designs, choose colours
with high contrast. So long as you
follow this rule, you cannot go
too wrong in your colour choice.

The same colour design can
look dramatically different

depending on the value of the
background colour, as this swatch
demonstrates. A pattern will stand
out best when paired with a
background of a very different
value. When the background and
pattern colour are of a similar
value, the pattern may disappear.
A good way to check this is to
imagine the colours in
monochrome.

*This traditional Scandinavian design
(left) uses two colours with a high
contrast in value.*

USING TWO COLOURS

The same two colours can look very different, and stand out or recede, depending on their placement in the design. Consider which parts of your design you want to stand out and which you want to recede, but bear in mind that sometimes it is only by swatching that you will know!

Needless to say, then, that the same motif in two different colours changes the design again. Having a hard time choosing what colours to use? Start with your favourite colour and add another with a high contrast to it.

These swatches show the same design, worked in the same two colours, but the colours have been reversed, significantly altering the appearance. See how the red net seems to recede into the grey background at top, while the grey net jumps out.

Here, combining red with white creates a bright, airy look, while combining red with black lends heft and solidity to the same design.

USING MORE THAN TWO COLOURS IN A ROW

Knitting with more than two colours in a row is more complex but, if you like the effect, it will warrant the extra work. Start by adding just a dash of your third colour to a simple design. Once you have gained experience handling more than two yarns you may decide to attempt even more complex designs.

The addition of a single red stitch to this geometric motif radically transforms it from the fairly traditional design on page 51. Although every fourth round will require working three colours, it is worth it!

USING MORE THAN TWO COLOURS IN A DESIGN

There are a few ways of introducing additional colours into your designs without making your knitting much more complicated.

When additional colours are introduced, it is often as a single stripe, or when an entirely new pattern element begins. This makes the knitting simple to execute as it is fairly easy to manipulate two yarns.

To brighten a figurative design, you can add colour to different elements of the design. Though 'colourful', so long as there are just two colours in each round, the knitting remains simple.

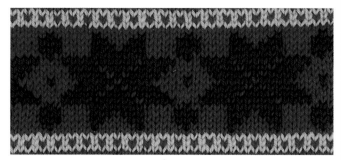

Add extra colours in bands or where a new pattern element begins.

This thistle uses three colours – to define the leaves, head and tip of the flower – but no more than two in a round.

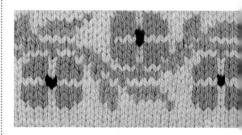

Here, almost every round of the pattern has three colours in use and on many rounds the distance between colour changes is quite long (creating long floats that will need weaving).

TRADITIONAL GARMENTS

It is often instructive to study the traditional garments of a culture in order to gather ideas for your own projects.

The origin of Scandinavian iconic designs is found in a number of places: sometimes in regional dress from the nineteenth century; occasionally a particular style can be traced back to a single individual's burst of inspiration; and in a couple of instances knitting co-operatives were responsible for the development of new styles or keeping old styles alive. Clearly, Scandinavian stranded knitting is a living, breathing art, changing and developing day by day.

In this class photo from Norway the children are dressed in many different arrangements of classic Scandinavian design elements; most are interpretations of a Lusekofte.

This nineteenth-century sweater is from the Hälsingland region of Sweden. Notice how the colour placement of the designs that span the chest divide the design at different points, fooling the eye into seeing two different designs.

LUSEKOFTE (LICE JACKETS): Norway

The folk of the Setesdal valley in Norway developed what is arguably the most recognizable Scandinavian sweater style, the lusekofte or lice jacket. It is named after the smallest pattern motif, a single colour stitch on a contrasting background. These are typically black sweaters patterned with many different white elements, usually including a 'kross og kringle' (cross and circle) at the shoulders and a ground of lice on the body.

FANA SWEATER: Norway

The Fana sweater features a classic arrangement of checkerboard bottom, followed by stripes with lice, and finished with eight-pointed roses or stars at the shoulders.

SELBUVOTTER (SELBU MITTENS): Norway

Marit Guldsetbrua Emstad is known as the 'Mother of Selbu Knitting'. She was born in 1841 and as a teenager, greatly influenced by the textile patterns around her, she experimented with placing a natural black 'Selburose' or eight-pointed rose (also recognised as a star) on a natural white background. Her designs were a hit in the neighbourhood, so her sisters and neighbours began to work these patterns and started selling them in nearby Trondheim. This mitten became part of the folk costume of the area, eventually becoming an important export of the region.

ALLOVER SWEATERS: Sweden

Knitters of the Hälsingland region of Sweden, which includes Delsbo and Bjuråker, produced interesting sweaters with very large allover patterns. It takes a person steeped in the decorative textile arts of the region to instantly understand the patterns, but with practice they begin to make sense. With large spaces between colour changes, they are knit at a very tight tension to mimic a woven fabric, or knit with the twined knitting technique called 'tvåändsstickning', which eliminates floats altogether.

BOHUS STICKNING: Sweden

Bohus Stickning began as a knitting co-operative in 1939 to provide relief work to the women of the economically hard-hit, stone-cutting region of Bohuslän, Sweden. It evolved over thirty years to become a house of high-fashion knitwear worn by elite women of the world. Designer and director Emma Jacobsson hired other talented designers to keep the brand fresh; for example, Kerstin Olsson, who is best known for her luxurious yoked sweaters that incorporate purl stitches into the colourwork patterns and are sometimes worked with a blend of wool and angora yarns. Jacobsson also revived interest in the local landrace sheep while searching for the perfect fibres for the co-operative.

BINGE (NOW HALLAND KNITTING COOPERATIVE): Sweden

Binge was established in 1907 to provide relief work to women of the Halland region of Sweden. It strived to preserve some of the

local traditional pattern designs. Gradually the co-operative grew to employ as many as 100 professional knitters. Garments were knit in various combinations of white, red and blue.

NATTRØJER (NIGHTSHIRTS): Denmark

Traditional Danish sweaters, though knit in a solid colour, use many of the same designs as stranded knitting but picked out in purl stitches on a plain stocking-stitch ground called 'damask knitting'. These 'damask' garments are closely related to knitted 'nightshirts' found all over northern Europe during the seventeenth and eighteenth centuries. Not always meant for sleeping in, 'nightshirt' was merely the name of a ubiquitous garment, worn by people of all classes, that was gradually incorporated into the national dress of the region.

ISLANDER SWEATERS: Faroe

In the Faroe Islands, thought to mean 'sheep islands', wool was so important to the economy that it was referred to as Faroese Gold! They are known for knitting sweaters with small allover repeat patterns often worked in natural colours. Faroe made a brisk trade in fishermen's sweaters knit with these small patterns using fairly thick yarn, confusingly often called Islanders. Fine work was reserved for family member's garments and folk costume.

LOPAPEYSA: Iceland

Though colour patterned knitting can be documented as far back as 1695, Lopapeysa, the iconic Icelandic sweater is quite young! Dating from the 1950s, this practical garment was possibly inspired by 'Eskimo' sweater patterns found in Danish and Norwegian knitting magazines in the mid-1950s. Clearly inspired by the beaded collars of Greenlanders folk costume, these yoked sweaters feature evenly spaced decreases that are incorporated as part of the pattern. Fashioned from Icelandic lopi yarn, they are instantly recognised as

'Icelandic' the world over. When knit from the plates of un-spun roving, the resulting sweater is an amazingly warm, yet incredibly light, garment perfectly suited for the climate. Visiting Iceland today, it is great fun to see all the people of both sexes and all ages wearing different versions of this sweater.

KORSNÄS: Finland

The Korsnäs is an unusual garment from the western islands of Finland that combines tapestry crochet worked in the same pattern designs as found in knitting, followed by a stocking-stitch ground of lice, and finished at the shoulders with more tapestry crochet. This interesting garment is great inspiration for today's craft revival, which often combines different needlework techniques in the same project.

These modern gloves from Selbu Husflid feature an eight-pointed star on a white background.

USING DESIGNS

A quick flip through this book will reveal how varied your use of these designs can be in your knitting. Each page is composed of several designs combined together. Sometimes they are arranged in an all-over pattern, sometimes vertically, horizontally and even diagonally!

All the patterns, even the very complex-looking ones are made up of smaller elements. I like to think of them as building blocks. You can use them as shown or mix them up a little.

The more you use the designs, the more you will understand them and see how they fit together like pieces of a jigsaw puzzle. By changing just one or two elements, you will open yourself up to enormous variation and endless possibilities for new designs.

Below are a few suggestions as to how to get started. Begin your experiments with small pattern repeats, and then build up to more complex ones.

CREATE NEW PATTERNS FROM SMALLER ELEMENTS

You will find that the smaller elements, when put together in different ways, can create entirely 'new' patterns.

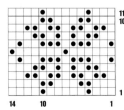

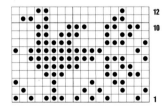

The tail feathers of the birds of design 126, when reflected and multiplied, become the star design on the hat on page 154.

CHANGE THE ORIENTATION

You could simply try turning a design on its head. Vertical designs can be worked horizontally (and vice versa) and look surprisingly different, especially in the context of a garment.

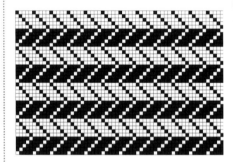

Imagine these chevrons worked on the sleeve or body of a sweater and the different effects they would have.

OFFSET THE DESIGNS

Offsetting designs is very simple to do, yet creates completely different arrangements, even with plain geometric designs.

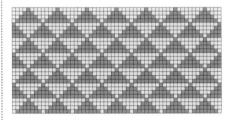

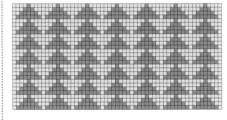

Offsetting the triangles of design 18, changes the pattern from a diamond one to a sequence of chevrons. Changing the colours transforms the pattern again (for more about colour see pages 30–31) – this is the pattern for the cowl on page 156.

EXPERIMENT WITHIN DESIGNS

If you are using a design with a strong, distinctive outline, you can experiment within that shape to create variety.

The centre of each of the flowers is different, creating a varied effect from a uniform design.

HELPFUL DESIGNS

Use friendly and familiar small geometric designs where there would otherwise be a long stretch between colours. This will eliminate difficult knitting by reducing the size of the floats, and is a common Scandinavian stranded knitting technique.

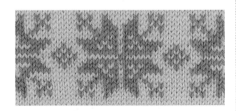

The simple diamonds in between these snowflakes make the knitting easier by reducing the length of the floats.

FIGURATIVE DESIGNS

Geometric patterns are not the only ones that can be toyed with. Having sets of animals marching in different directions across your knitting creates dynamism and movement. Alternatively, having animals turn toward each other can be used to tell different stories.

The reindeer (top) majestically face each other, as if in battle, whereas the doves that face each other, interspersed with hearts (bottom) seem to look lovingly into each others' eyes.

The goats marching to the right and horses leaping to the left (above) send the eye in different directions, creating movement.

TRANSITION DESIGNS

When making a transition between background colours, it can be fun to mark the break with a small repeat design. This also helps to soften what could be a stark transition. Small transitional designs are also a great place to introduce an additional colour.

The transition designs soften the change of background colour and add texture and interest to the composition.

The transition designs introduce an extra colour.

PLANNING A PROJECT

This book is first and foremost a collection of pattern designs. Although it is beyond the scope of this book to teach the nuances of Scandinavian garment design, here are some ideas for using the patterns in your own projects.

For all projects, careful planning is the key to success. Here, we use the example of a sweater, but the steps apply to any project. Even if you are knitting a simple pair of mittens, it is a good idea to draw some initial design sketches, take measurements, knit a tension swatch, and check the fit of the stitches and rows.

The designs in this book can be used in multiple ways on all sorts of different items.

1 INITIAL QUESTIONS

Ask yourself the following questions before you start any project.

WHAT DO YOU WANT TO MAKE?

First of all, you must decide what you want to make. A hat, an afghan, a pullover or a cardigan? A pillow, a pincushion, a bag or some socks? The item you want to make will help narrow down what pattern designs you would like to use and how you want to apply them.

TIP

Since Scandinavian knitting is most commonly and easily knitted in the round, a good place to start is a knitted tube. if you have a moment of genius in the first few pattern repeats, you can turn your tube into a hat; if you continue knitting but end up with something you wouldn't wear, you can make your tube into a draft excluder, a small bolster cushion or a hand warmer; if you are enjoying experimenting you can continue knitting until your tube is 1m (3ft) long, when you will have a cosy scarf. Whatever you decide, you will have made a tension swatch and a stitch pattern test swatch that you can use to plan other projects.

WHAT IS ITS PURPOSE?

Next you need to determine the purpose of the item, which will help you decide which designs are best suited for the item. Does it need to be sturdy and hold up to a lot of wear and tear? If so, you may want to use small, simple motifs that create a dense textile and are not difficult to knit. Or will it be more of a fashion item for show? If so, it may be worth your while including more elaborate, complicated designs.

HOW MUCH TIME?

Decide how much work you would like to devote to your project. Simple projects with easy-to-memorise motifs in only two colours might be the perfect project to bring to a lively knitting group. A complicated asymmetric or large pattern might be best suited to individual knitting time by the fireside during long winter nights. Even more complicated designs will require careful following of a chart, meaning aids like post-it notes and excellent lighting conditions.

Formulate ideas by executing a number of rough sketches – think about pattern placement and how many colours you are comfortable using at one time.

TIP
To experiment with pattern placement, try photocopying the designs in this book, cutting them into strips and placing them next to each other. Try different arrangements: you might decide you need to introduce an extra pattern to give your garment balance. You will get a good idea of which designs look good together, how many times to use a pattern, and what kind of centring you will need.

2 DESIGN IDEAS

Once you have decided what to make, you can start choosing designs and deciding how to put them together.

Take inspiration from this book, your yarn stash, particular colours, previous projects – wherever you can find it – to generate some initial ideas and draw some rough sketches

Consider the placement of your designs: Will they run horizontally, vertically or as an allover arrangement? Will there be a central, focal point? Or will the motifs repeat all the way round?

Also think about whether you are comfortable with using more than two colours in a round. If not, introduce colour at a break in the pattern sequence, not within a single motif.

Once you've got an idea of what you like, take the time to swatch to see if the knitted piece is as successful as your drawing.

Approach this task with a sense of adventure and don't be afraid to try something entirely new; Scandinavian design is, after all, both innovative and creative.

Use your final sketch to make notes as you mull the project over and proceed with the design process.

TIP
When using large patterns with many stitches between colour changes, you may decide to shorten the long floats by inserting one or two stitches in between.

3 TAKE YOUR MEASUREMENTS

Accurate measurements are the key to success, so note all important measurements on your sketch. For a sweater, measure the following:

- Bust/chest circumference (**1**)
- Back length – nape of neck to waist or hip (**2**)
- Sleeve length, wrist to underarm (**3**)
- Armhole depth (**4**)
- Neckline width (**5**)
- Wrist circumference (**6**)
- Hem circumference (**7**)

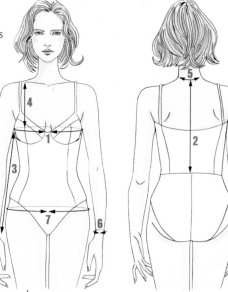

ADAPTING AN EXISTING PATTERN

Rather than designing an entire garment from scratch, adapting an existing pattern is a good starting point. By swapping out motifs and choosing your own colour scheme, you can produce a totally unique garment, as well as practise some of the guiding principles of Scandinavian design.

Start by knitting a tension swatch as you would if you were knitting the pattern as described. If you are substituting the yarn, then work the swatch in the yarn you plan to use but using the stitch pattern combinations of the project pattern. This will give you a feel for the pattern and ideas of how you may like to adapt it for your own project.

There are three points to consider when substituting yarns and patterns in a design:

Tension: The tension of your yarn must exactly match those specified in the instructions.

Pattern repeat: To make the process an easy one, your chosen patterns must fit exactly into the total number of stitches in the garment.

Row count: The number of rows in your selected designs must correspond to those making up the garment's length.

4 DETERMINE YOUR TENSION

Knit a generous tension swatch (see pages 14–15), using the type of yarn, the designs and the needle size you intend to use for the finished piece.

Pay special attention to the number of plain rows of knitting in your piece. Plain knitting produces a row tension greater than the stitch tension, so make sure your swatch has the same ratio of plain rows to stranded rows as your planned garment. This tension swatch will determine all your final calculations.

Tension swatch stitches	32 stitches to 10cm (4in)
Stitches per cm (inch)	8 stitches to 2.5cm (1in)
Sweater size	45-cm (18in) chest × 2 (for front and back) = 90-cm (36in) circumference
Total number of stitches for width	8 stitches × 36 = 288 stitches

5 DETERMINE THE NUMBER OF STITCHES FOR THE WIDTH

To work out how many stitches you need to cast on, multiply the required width of your garment by two (you'll be knitting in the round and need to cast on enough stitches for both the front and the back at the same time). Then multiply this number by the number of stitches in 2.5cm (1in) of your tension swatch.

For example, if your stitch tension comes out at 32 stitches to 10cm (4in), and you want your sweater to fit a 90-cm (36in) chest, multiply 90-cm (36in) by 8 (the number of stitches in 2.5cm/1in).

Tension swatch rows	32 rows to 10cm (4in)
Rows per cm (inch)	8 rows to 2.5cm (1in)
Sweater size	50cm (20in)
Total number of rows for length	8 rows × 20 = 160 rows

6 DETERMINE THE NUMBER OF ROWS FOR THE LENGTH

To find the total length, multiply the length you want the garment to be by the number of rows in 2.5cm (1in) of the tension swatch. For example, if your stitch tension comes out at 32 rows to 10cm (4in), and you want your sweater to be 50cm (20in) long, multiply 50cm (20in) by 8 (the number of rows in 2.5cm/1in).

Then, repeat these calculations for all parts of the garment noted on your sketch.

7 CHECK THE MATHS OF YOUR DESIGNS

The number of pattern repeats in your chosen designs must fit into the total number of stitches. So if the total number of stitches is 140, then you can use patterns with repeats of 2, 4, 5, 7, 10, 14, and 20. Similarly, the number of rows must fit into the total length.

If the pattern repeat does not fit exactly, you have a few options: you can adjust it (see box, left), choose another, similar, motif or change the total number of stitches of the garment, provided this will not change the size of your finished garment too much.

It is easier to adjust the number of rows in a garment as it is possible to add in rows of plain knitting between designs or create a band of corrugated ribbing.

Make a chart on graph paper of your final design. The red lines show where the neckline will be and the blue lines plot the designs that will be worked for the sleeves.

8 PLACING PATTERN DESIGNS

To centre a pattern, the midpoint of the design must be placed at the centre front stitch of the garment. With an even number of repeats, the back and front will not have complete designs on them. This means the beginning of the round will need to be adjusted accordingly. If the number of repeats is odd, the back and front will have complete repeats on them, but they will not match at the shoulders. To compensate, a lice pattern can be worked at the shoulder join to camouflage this.

Vertical arrangements should end at the shoulder with a complete design or at the centre of a design.

9 FINAL DESIGN

Finally, write up all your adjustments and calculations. Redraw your sketch with all the correct measurements and with a reminder of where any steeks will be placed and how many stitches they will be. Make a chart of the final pattern designs on graph paper with the correct placement. It is also useful to tape strands of yarn to the side of the chart, labelled with their shade number, so that you can see instantly which yarn to use and when.

This sweater has geometric patterning circling the yoke, wrists and lower edge.

ADJUSTING STITCH REPEATS

Sometimes the stitch pattern you'd like to use won't fit perfectly into the number of stitches needed for your project; make patterns fit by adjusting stitch repeats.

For example, Design 106, a 10 round 14 stitch repeat, can easily be adjusted by eliminating or adding smaller designs between the heart shape. (see right).

Experiment with reducing and enlarging other designs on graph paper.

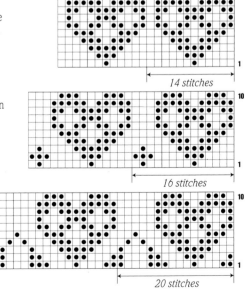

14 stitches

16 stitches

20 stitches

DESIGN
DIRECTORY

The design directory begins with a colourful visual selector displaying all the designs side by side. Flip through for inspiration and to choose your design, then turn to the relevant page to create your chosen design. The directory itself includes a stunning, actual-size photograph, a black-and-white chart, a colour chart and a colour-variation chart for each of the 150 designs.

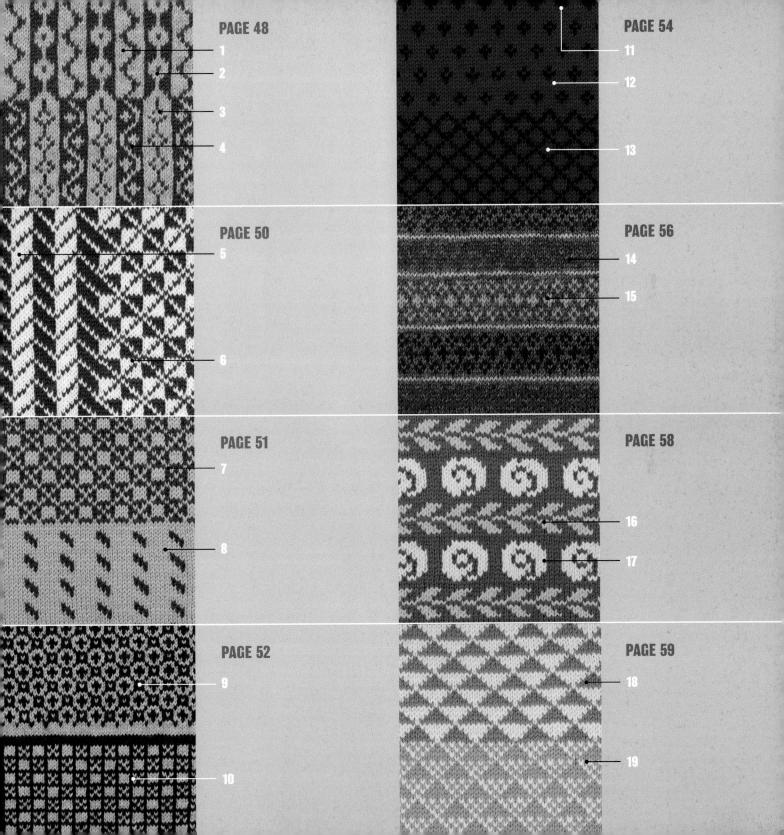

PAGE 48
1
2
3
4

PAGE 50
5
6

PAGE 51
7
8

PAGE 52
9
10

PAGE 54
11
12
13

PAGE 56
14
15

PAGE 58
16
17

PAGE 59
18
19

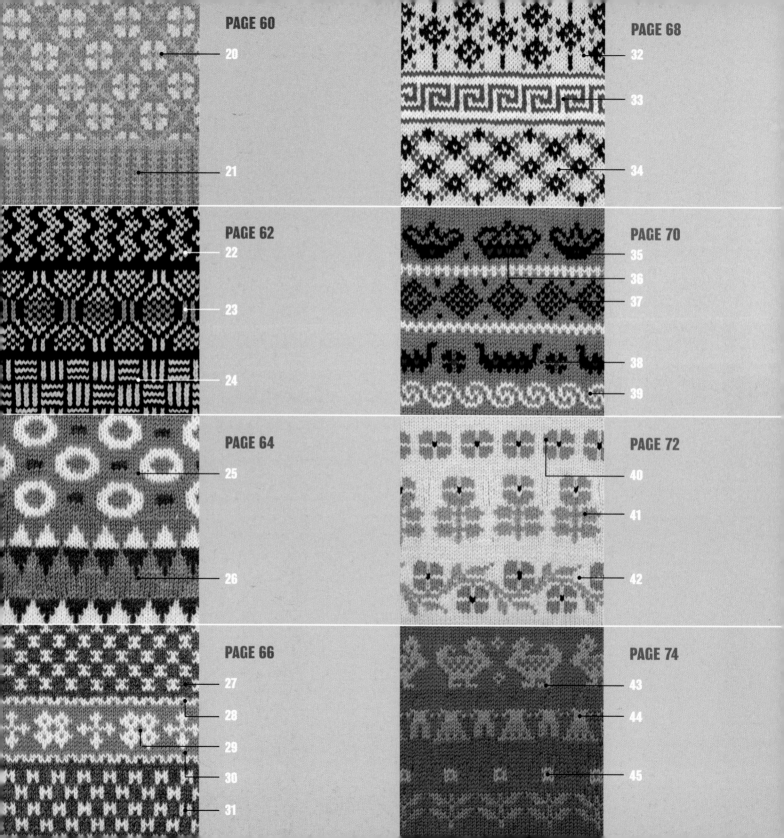

PAGE 60

20

21

PAGE 68

32

33

34

PAGE 62

22

23

24

PAGE 70

35

36

37

38

39

PAGE 64

25

26

PAGE 72

40

41

42

PAGE 66

27

28

29

30

31

PAGE 74

43

44

45

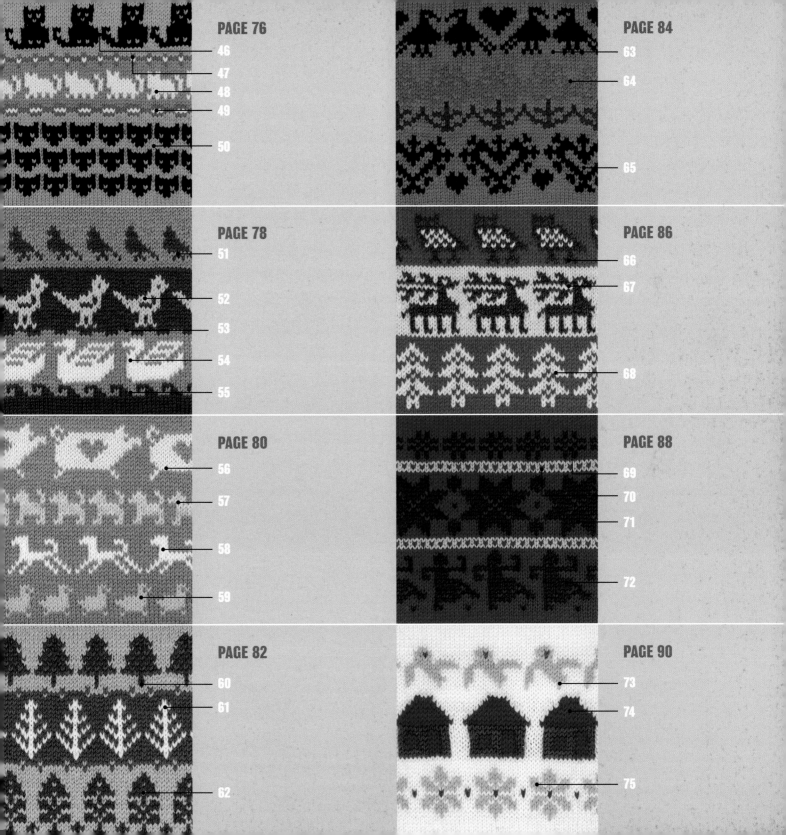

PAGE 76
46
47
48
49
50

PAGE 84
63
64
65

PAGE 78
51
52
53
54
55

PAGE 86
66
67
68

PAGE 80
56
57
58
59

PAGE 88
69
70
71
72

PAGE 82
60
61
62

PAGE 90
73
74
75

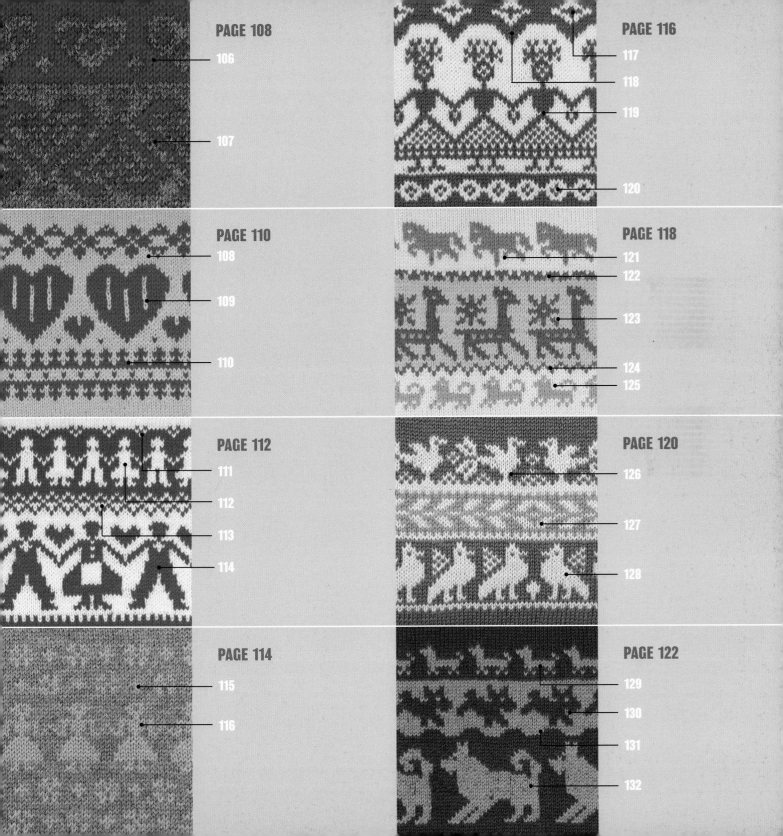

PAGE 108

106

107

PAGE 116

117

118

119

120

PAGE 110

108

109

110

PAGE 118

121

122

123

124

125

PAGE 112

111

112

113

114

PAGE 120

126

127

128

PAGE 114

115

116

PAGE 122

129

130

131

132

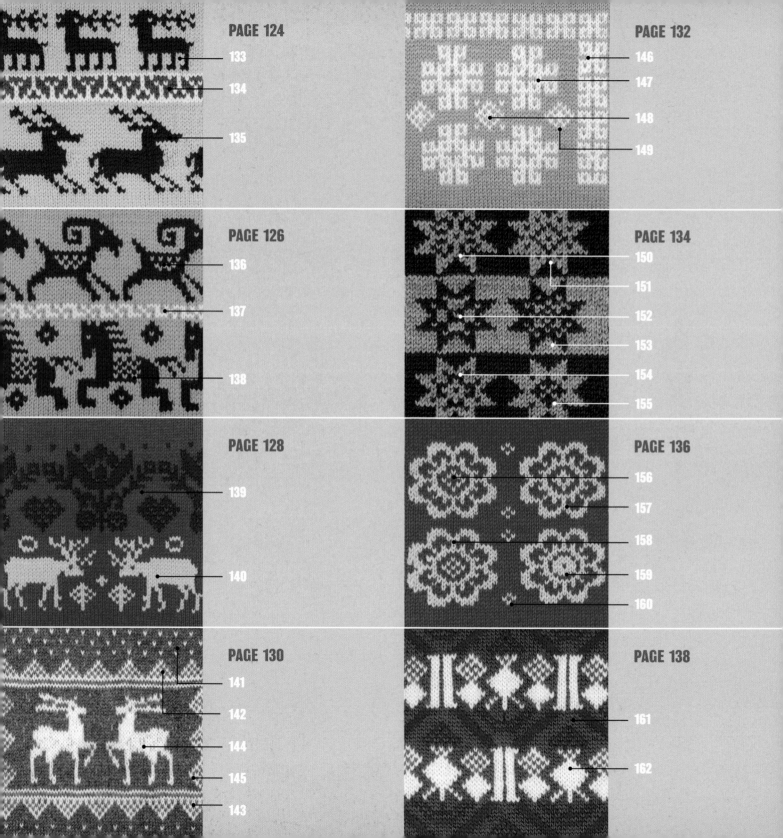

PAGE 124
133
134
135

PAGE 132
146
147
148
149

PAGE 126
136
137
138

PAGE 134
150
151
152
153
154
155

PAGE 128
139
140

PAGE 136
156
157
158
159
160

PAGE 130
141
142
144
145
143

PAGE 138
161
162

8 ROWS
7 STITCHES

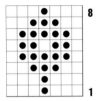

Black-and-white chart
for swatch

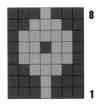

Colour chart for swatch

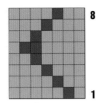

Colour-variation chart

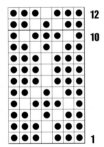

8 ROWS
7 STITCHES

Black-and-white chart
for swatch

Colour chart for swatch

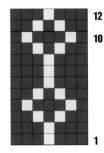

Colour-variation chart

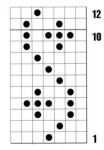

12 ROWS
7 STITCHES

Black-and-white chart
for swatch

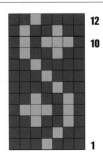

Colour chart for swatch

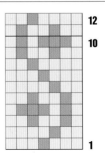

Colour-variation chart

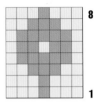

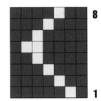

12 ROWS
7 STITCHES

Black-and-white chart
for swatch

Colour chart for swatch

Colour-variation chart

5

5 ROWS
10 STITCHES

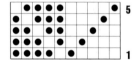

Black-and-white chart for swatch

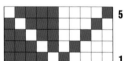

Colour chart for swatch

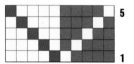

Colour-variation chart

6

10 ROWS
10 STITCHES

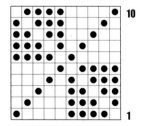

Black-and-white chart for swatch

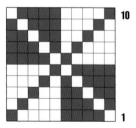

Colour chart for swatch

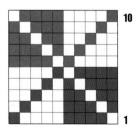

Colour-variation chart

Black-and-white chart
for swatch

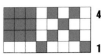

Colour chart for swatch

Colour-variation chart·

4 ROWS
8 STITCHES

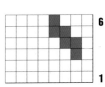

Black-and-white chart
for swatch

Colour chart for swatch

Colour-variation chart

6 ROWS
8 STITCHES

9

8 ROWS
8 STITCHES

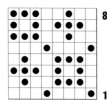

Black-and-white chart
for swatch

Colour chart
for swatch

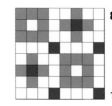

Colour-variation
chart

10

8 ROWS
8 STITCHES

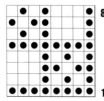

Black-and-white chart
for swatch

Colour chart
for swatch

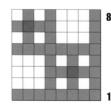

Colour-variation
chart

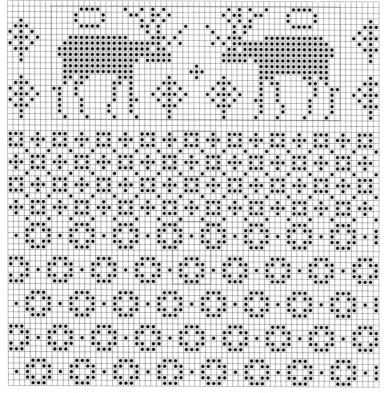

Mix and match
motifs 140 + 9 + 10

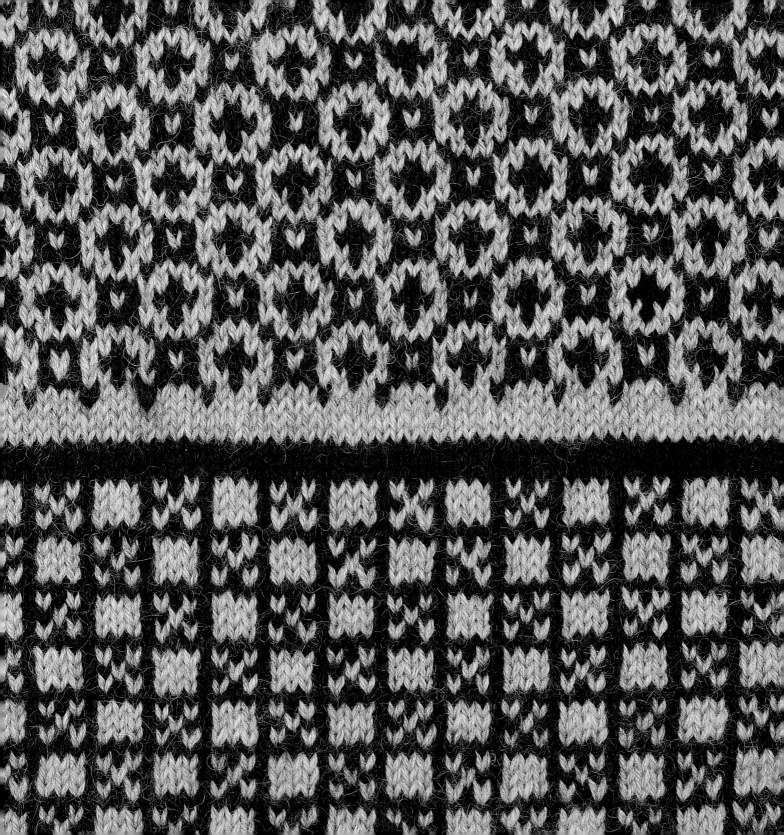

11

8 ROWS
6 STITCHES

Black-and-white
chart for swatch

Colour chart
for swatch

Colour-variation
chart

12

12 ROWS
6 STITCHES

Black-and-white
chart for swatch

Colour chart
for swatch

Colour-variation
chart

13

6 ROWS
6 STITCHES

Black-and-white
chart for swatch

Colour chart
for swatch

Colour-variation
chart

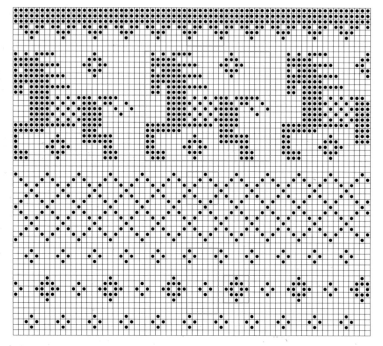

Mix and match motifs
11 + 138 + 13 + 12

14

10 ROWS
12 STITCHES

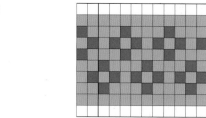

Black-and-white chart for swatch

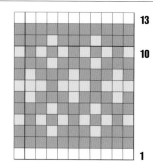

Colour chart for swatch

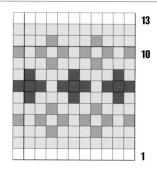

Colour-variation chart

15

13 ROWS
11 STITCHES

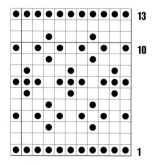

Black-and-white chart for swatch

Colour chart for swatch

Colour-variation chart

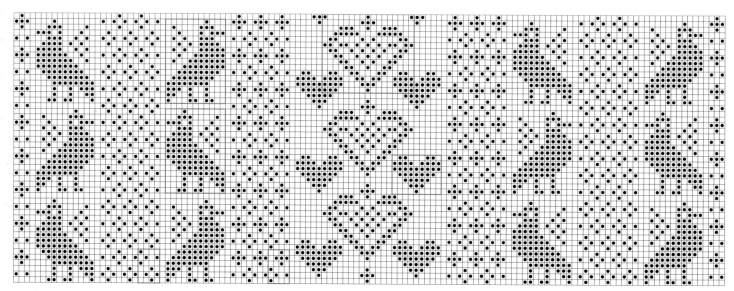

Mix and match motifs 14 + 128 + 15 + 65

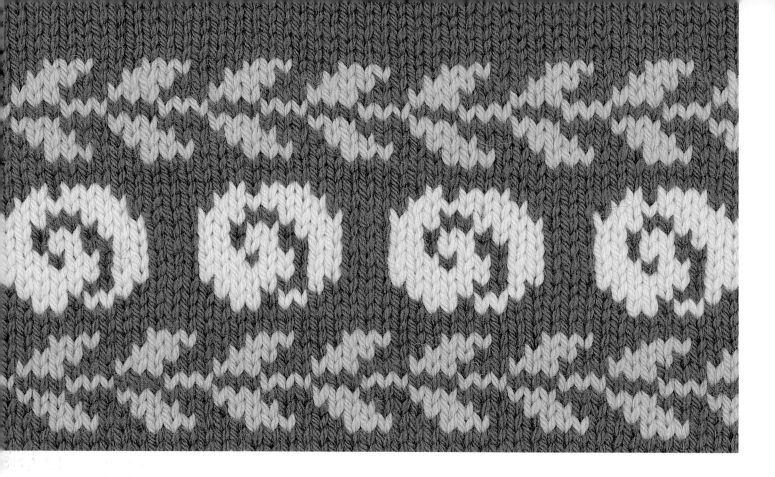

16

7 ROWS
6 STITCHES

Black-and-white
chart for swatch

Colour chart for swatch

Colour-variation chart

17

9 ROWS
12 STITCHES

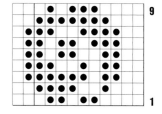 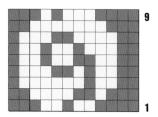 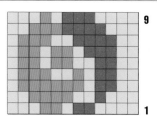

Black-and-white chart for swatch

Colour chart for swatch

Colour-variation chart

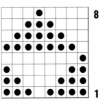

Black-and-white
chart for swatch

8 ROWS
8 STITCHES

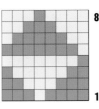

Colour chart
for swatch

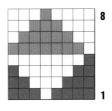

Colour-
variation chart

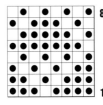

Black-and-white
chart for swatch

8 ROWS
8 STITCHES

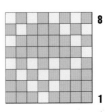

Colour chart
for swatch

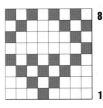

Colour-variation
chart

20

16 ROWS
14 STITCHES

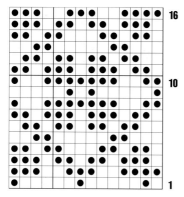

Black-and-white chart for swatch

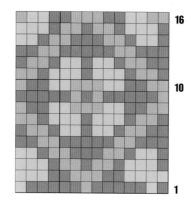

Colour chart for swatch

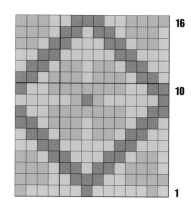

Colour-variation chart

21

2 ROWS
4 STITCHES

Black-and-white
chart for swatch

Colour chart
for swatch

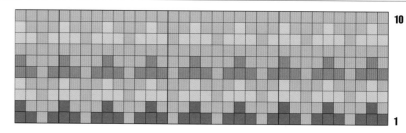

Colour and row repeat variation chart

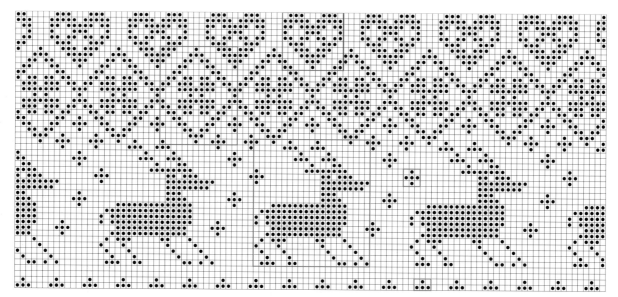

Mix and match motifs 106 + 20 + 135 + 92 + 21

60

22

6 ROWS
6 STITCHES

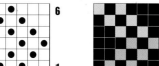

Black-and-white chart
for swatch

Colour chart for swatch

Colour-variation chart

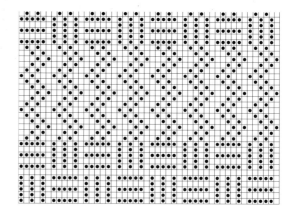

Mix and match charts 22 + 24

23

19 ROWS
14 STITCHES

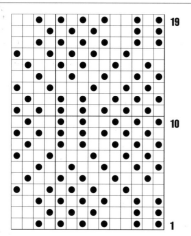

Black-and-white chart for swatch

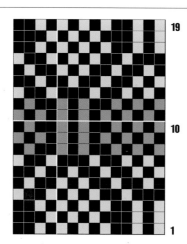

Colour chart for swatch

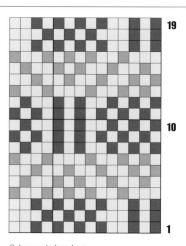

Colour-variation chart

24

12 ROWS
12 STITCHES

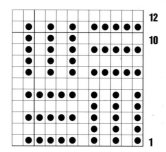

Black-and-white chart for swatch

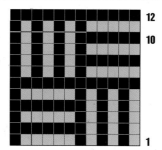

Colour chart for swatch

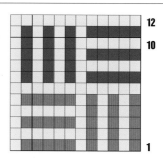

Colour-variation chart

25

27 **ROWS**
18 **STITCHES**

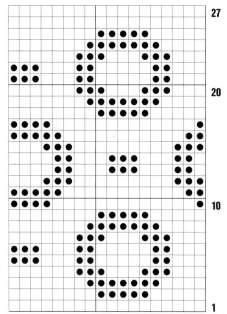

Black-and-white chart for swatch

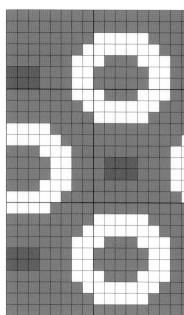

Colour chart for swatch

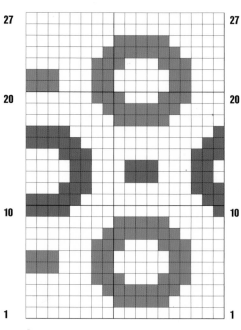

Colour-variation chart

26

24 **ROWS**
6 **STITCHES**

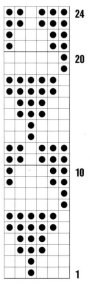

Black-and-white
chart for swatch

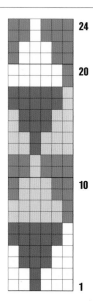

Colour chart
for swatch

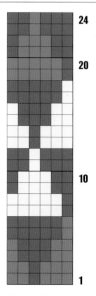

Colour-variation
chart

27

3 ROWS
6 STITCHES

 3
1

Black-and-white
chart for swatch

 3
1

Colour chart for swatch

 3
1

Colour-variation chart

28

2 ROWS
4 STITCHES

 2
1

Black-and-white
chart for swatch

 2
1

Colour chart for swatch

2
1

Colour-variation chart

29

9 ROWS
10 STITCHES

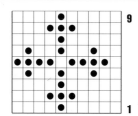 9
1

Black-and-white chart for swatch

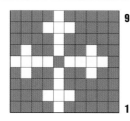 9
1

Colour chart for swatch

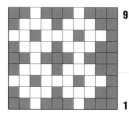 9
1

Colour-variation chart

30

9 ROWS
10 STITCHES

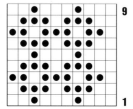 9
1

Black-and-white chart for swatch

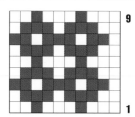 9
1

Colour chart for swatch

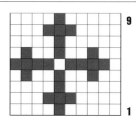 9
1

Colour-variation chart

31

3 ROWS
6 STITCHES

 3
1

Black-and-white
chart for swatch

 3
1

Colour chart for swatch

 3
1

Colour-variation chart

66

32

15 ROWS
16 STITCHES

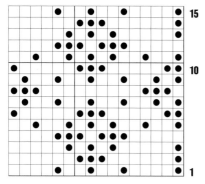

Black-and-white chart for swatch

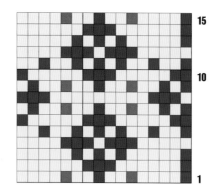

Colour chart for swatch

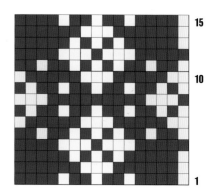

Colour-variation chart

33

12 ROWS
8 STITCHES

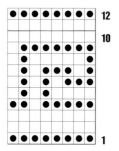

Black-and-white chart for swatch

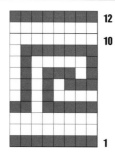

Colour chart for swatch

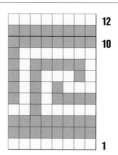

Colour-variation chart

34

17 ROWS
12 STITCHES

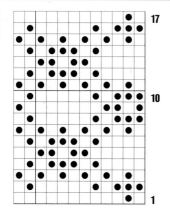

Black-and-white chart for swatch

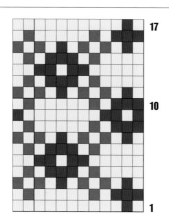

Colour chart for swatch

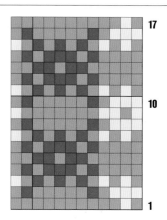

Colour-variation chart

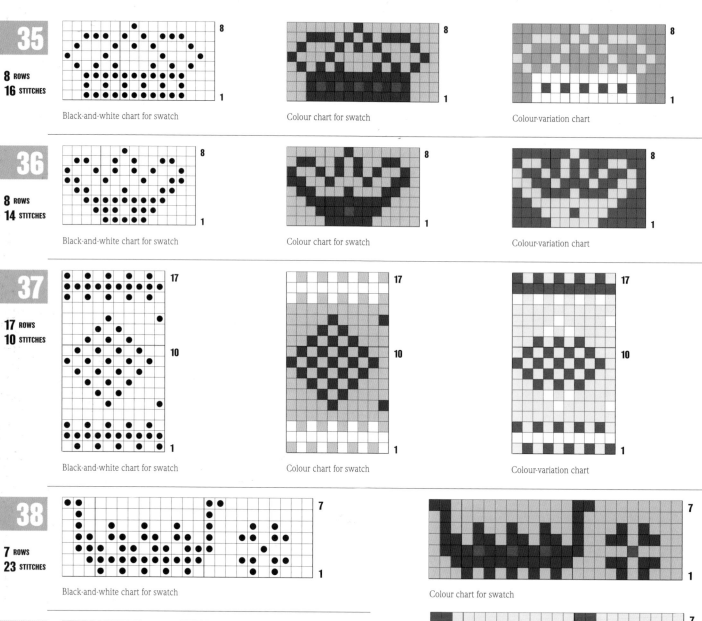

40

7 ROWS
9 STITCHES

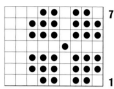

Black-and-white chart for swatch

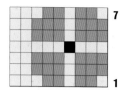

Colour chart for swatch

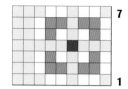

Colour-variation chart

41

16 ROWS
13 STITCHES

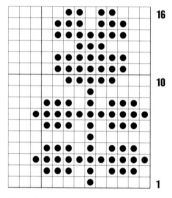

Black-and-white chart for swatch

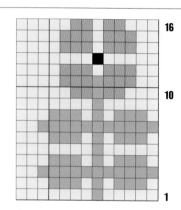

Colour chart for swatch

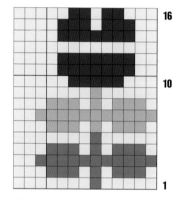

Colour-variation chart

42

13 ROWS
20 STITCHES

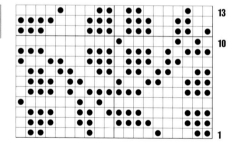

Black-and-white chart for swatch

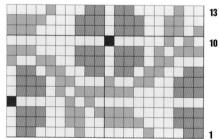

Colour chart for swatch

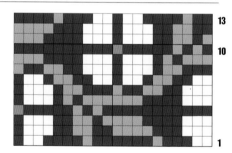

Colour-variation chart

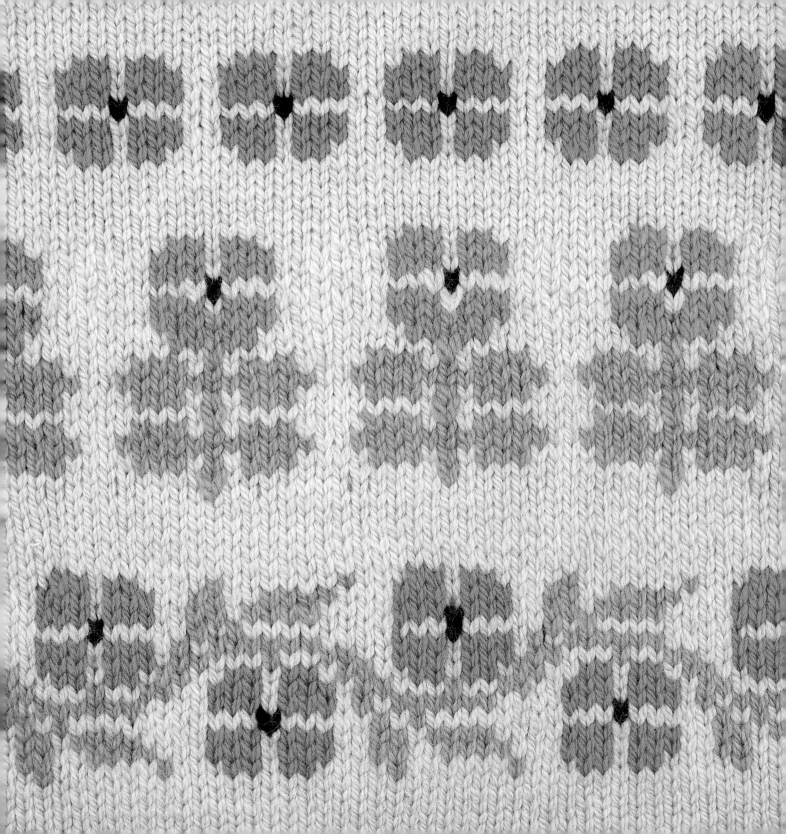

43

13 ROWS
16 STITCHES

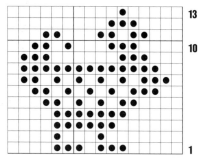

Black-and-white chart for swatch

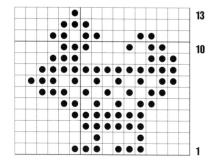

Black-and-white chart for swatch

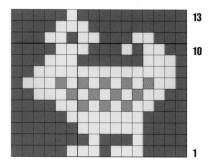

Colour chart for swatch

44

14 ROWS
16 STITCHES

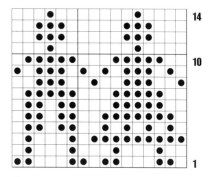

Black-and-white chart for swatch

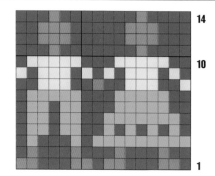

Colour chart for swatch

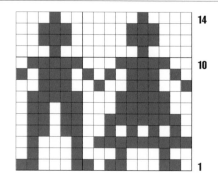

Colour-variation chart

45

18 ROWS
12 STITCHES

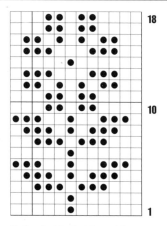

Black-and-white chart for swatch

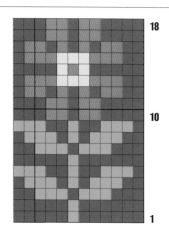

Colour chart for swatch

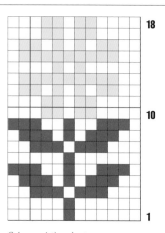

Colour-variation chart

46

11 ROWS
12 STITCHES

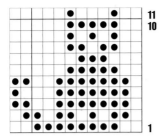
Black-and-white chart for swatch

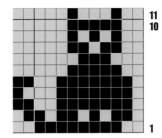
Colour chart for swatch

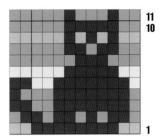
Colour-variation chart

47

3 ROWS
4 STITCHES

Black-and-white chart for swatch

Colour chart for swatch

Colour-variation chart

48

7 ROWS
10 STITCHES

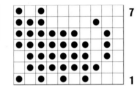
Black-and-white chart for swatch

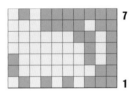
Colour chart for swatch

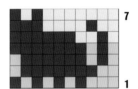
Colour-variation chart

49

3 ROWS
6 STITCHES

Black-and-white chart for swatch

Colour chart for swatch

Colour-variation chart

50

6 ROWS
7 STITCHES

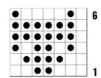
Black-and-white chart for swatch

Colour chart for swatch

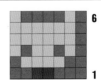
Colour-variation chart

51

8 ROWS
9 STITCHES

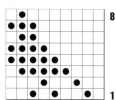

Black-and-white chart for swatch

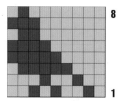

Colour chart for swatch

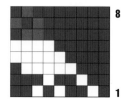

Colour-variation chart

52

13 ROWS
14 STITCHES

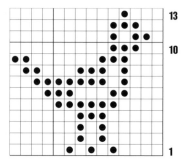

Black-and-white chart for swatch

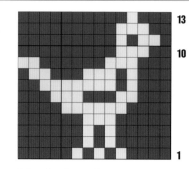

Colour chart for swatch

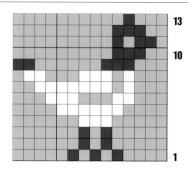

Colour-variation chart

53

1 ROWS
6 STITCHES

Black-and-white chart for swatch

Colour chart for swatch

Colour-variation chart

54

11 ROWS
16 STITCHES

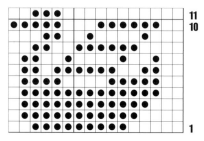

Black-and-white chart for swatch

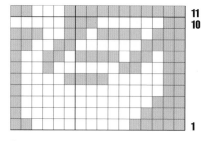

Colour chart for swatch

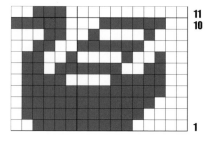

Colour-variation chart

55

4 ROWS
6 STITCHES

Black-and-white chart for swatch

Colour chart for swatch

Colour-variation chart

56

13 ROWS
22 STITCHES

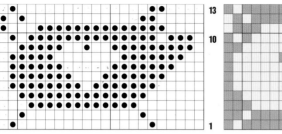

Black-and-white chart for swatch

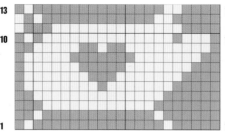

Colour chart for swatch

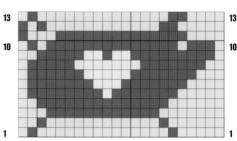

Colour-variation chart

57

7 ROWS
9 STITCHES

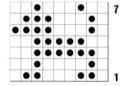

Black-and-white chart for swatch

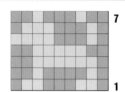

Colour chart for swatch

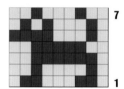

Colour-variation chart

58

9 ROWS
16 STITCHES

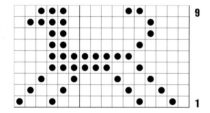

Black-and-white chart for swatch

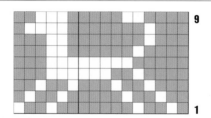

Colour chart for swatch

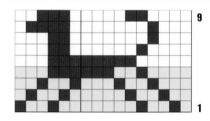

Colour-variation chart

59

8 ROWS
9 STITCHES

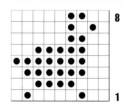

Black-and-white chart for swatch

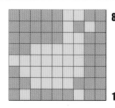

Colour chart for swatch

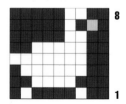

Colour-variation chart

60

11 ROWS
10 STITCHES

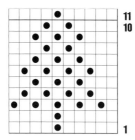

Black-and-white chart for swatch

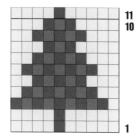

Colour chart for swatch

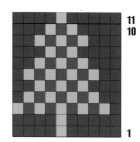

Colour-variation chart

61

16 ROWS
10 STITCHES

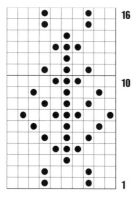

Black-and-white chart for swatch

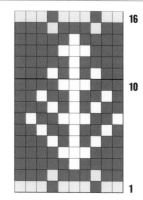

Colour chart for swatch

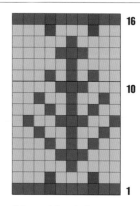

Colour-variation chart

62

15 ROWS
10 STITCHES

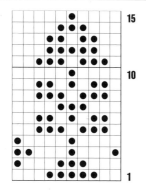

Black-and-white chart for swatch

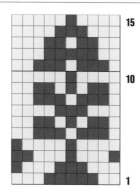

Colour chart for swatch

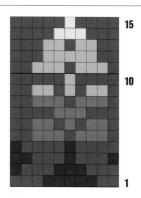

Colour-variation chart

63

12 ROWS
26 STITCHES

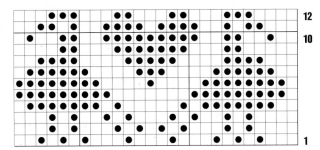

Black-and-white chart for swatch

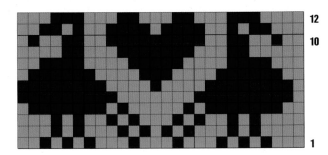

Colour chart for swatch

64

17 ROWS
12 STITCHES

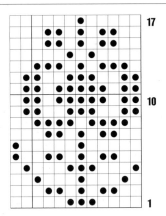

Black-and-white chart for swatch

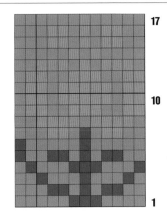

Colour chart for swatch

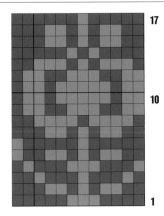

Colour-variation chart

65

14 ROWS
20 STITCHES

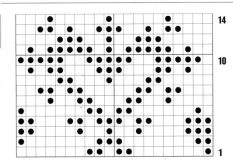

Black-and-white chart for swatch

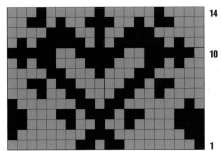

Colour chart for swatch

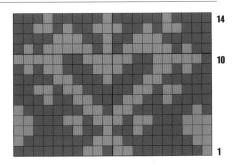

Colour-variation chart

66

12 ROWS
13 STITCHES

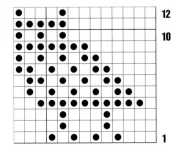

Black-and-white chart for swatch

Colour chart for swatch

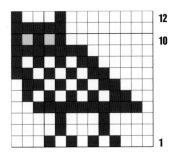

Colour-variation chart

67

15 ROWS
15 STITCHES

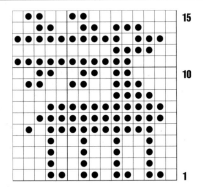

Black-and-white chart for swatch

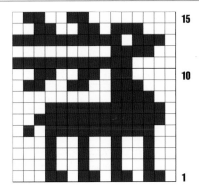

Colour chart for swatch

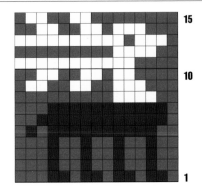

Colour-variation chart

68

15 ROWS
10 STITCHES

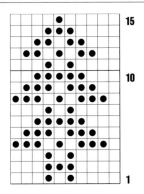

Black-and-white chart for swatch

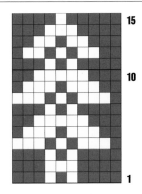

Colour chart for swatch

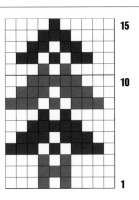

Colour-variation chart

69

7 ROWS
8 STITCHES

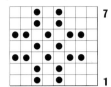

Black-and-white chart for swatch

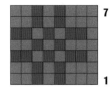

Colour chart for swatch

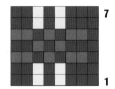

Colour-variation chart

70

3 ROWS
4 STITCHES

Black-and-white chart for swatch

Colour chart for swatch

Colour-variation chart

71

15 ROWS
18 STITCHES

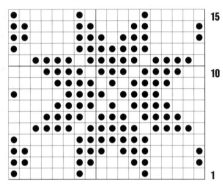

Black-and-white chart for swatch

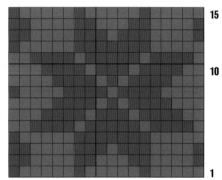

Colour chart for swatch

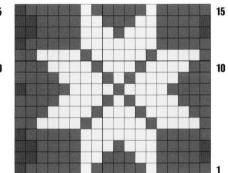

Colour-variation chart

72

15 ROWS
12 STITCHES

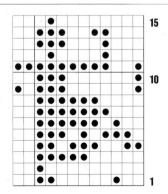

Black-and-white chart for swatch

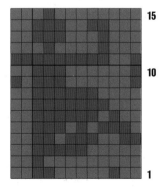

Colour chart for swatch

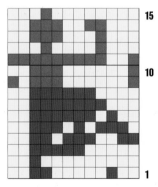

Colour-variation chart

73

9 ROWS
13 STITCHES

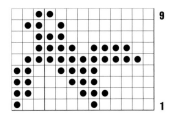

Black-and-white chart for swatch

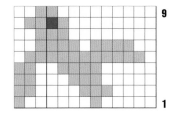

Colour chart for swatch

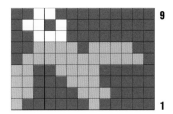

Colour-variation chart

74

13 ROWS
16 STITCHES

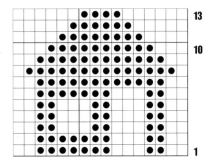

Black-and-white chart for swatch

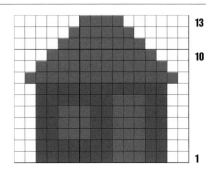

Colour chart for swatch

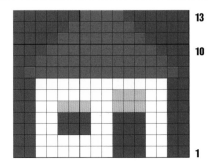

Colour-variation chart

75

11 ROWS
12 STITCHES

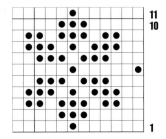

Black-and-white chart for swatch

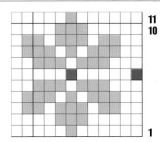

Colour chart for swatch

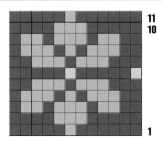

Colour-variation chart

76

12 ROWS
12 STITCHES

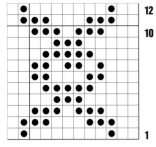

Black-and-white chart for swatch

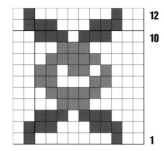

Colour chart for swatch

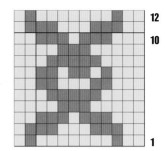

Colour-variation chart

77

11 ROWS
16 STITCHES

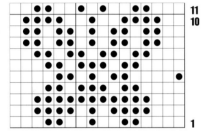

Black-and-white chart for swatch

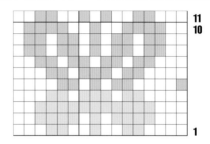

Colour chart for swatch

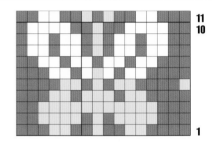

Colour-variation chart

78

21 ROWS
11 STITCHES

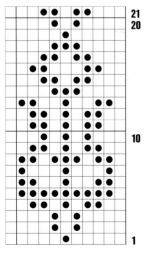

Black-and-white chart for swatch

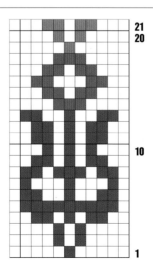

Colour chart for swatch

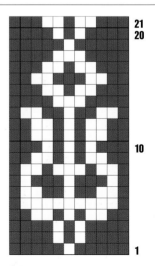

Colour-variation chart

79

9 ROWS
10 STITCHES

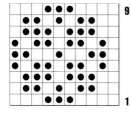

Black-and-white chart for swatch

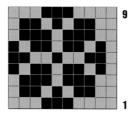

Colour chart for swatch

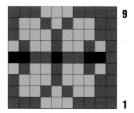

Colour-variation chart

80

11 ROWS
12 STITCHES

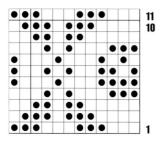

Black-and-white chart for swatch

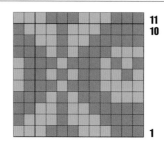

Colour chart for swatch

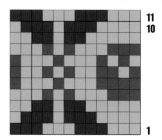

Colour-variation chart

81

12 ROWS
8 STITCHES

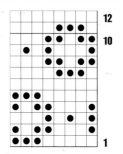

Black-and-white chart for swatch

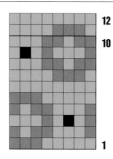

Colour chart for swatch

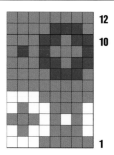

Colour-variation chart

82

11 ROWS
20 STITCHES

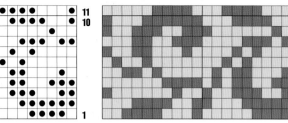

Black-and-white chart for swatch

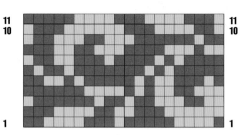

Colour chart for swatch

Colour-variation chart

83

7 ROWS
12 STITCHES

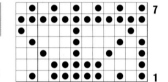

Black-and-white chart for swatch

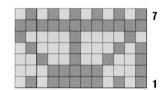

Colour chart for swatch

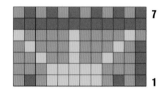

Colour-variation chart

84

10 ROWS
28 STITCHES

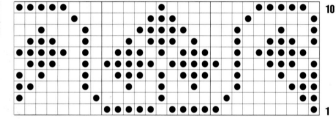

Black-and-white chart for swatch

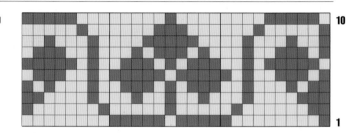

Colour chart for swatch

85

8 ROWS
32 STITCHES

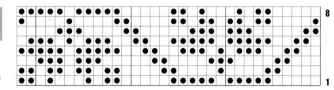

Black-and-white chart for swatch

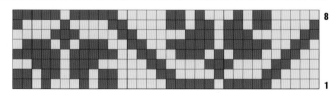

Colour chart for swatch

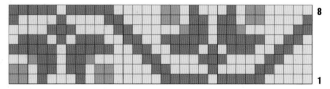

Colour-variation chart

86

6 ROWS
4 STITCHES

Black-and-white chart for swatch

Colour chart for swatch

Colour-variation chart

87

3 ROWS
8 STITCHES

Black-and-white chart for swatch

Colour chart for swatch

Colour-variation chart

88

21 ROWS
22 STITCHES

Black-and-white chart for swatch

Colour chart for swatch

Colour-variation chart

89

5 ROWS
4 STITCHES

Black-and-white chart for swatch

Colour chart for swatch

Colour-variation chart

90

5 ROWS
4 STITCHES

Black-and-white chart for swatch

Colour chart for swatch

Colour-variation chart

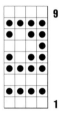

91

13 ROWS
12 STITCHES

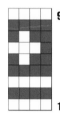

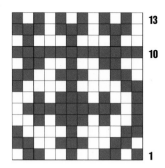

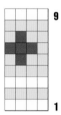

Black-and-white chart for swatch

Colour chart for swatch

Colour-variation chart

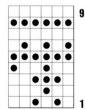

92

9 ROWS
4 STITCHES

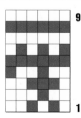

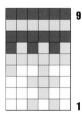

Black-and-white
chart for swatch

Colour chart
for swatch

Colour-variation
chart

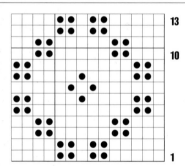

93

13 ROWS
14 STITCHES

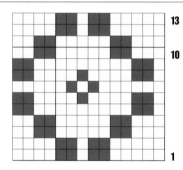

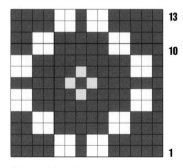

Black-and-white chart for swatch

Colour chart for swatch

Colour-variation chart

94

9 ROWS
6 STITCHES

Black-and-white
chart for swatch

Colour chart
for swatch

Colour-variation
chart

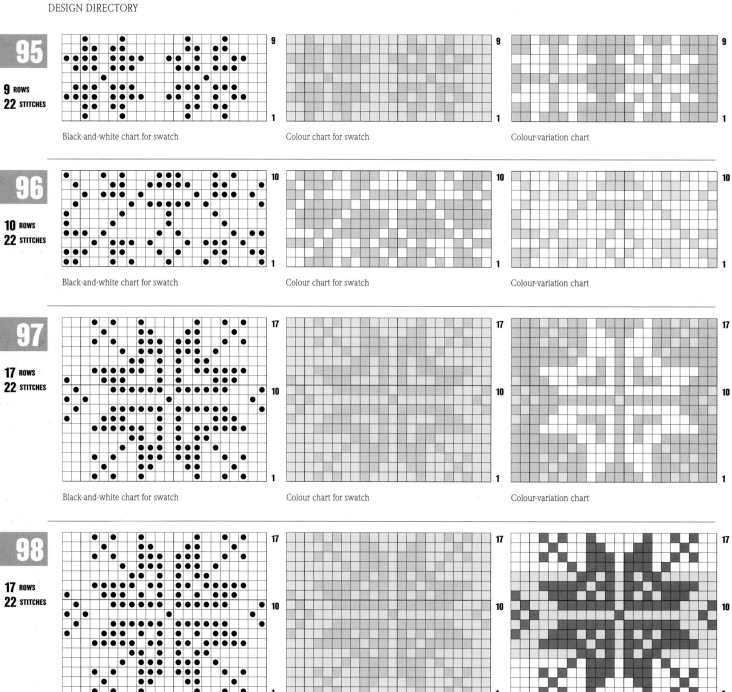

95

9 ROWS
22 STITCHES

Black-and-white chart for swatch

Colour chart for swatch

Colour-variation chart

96

10 ROWS
22 STITCHES

Black-and-white chart for swatch

Colour chart for swatch

Colour-variation chart

97

17 ROWS
22 STITCHES

Black-and-white chart for swatch

Colour chart for swatch

Colour-variation chart

98

17 ROWS
22 STITCHES

Black-and-white chart for swatch

Colour chart for swatch

Colour-variation chart

99

3 ROWS
8 STITCHES

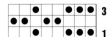 3
1
Black-and-white chart for swatch

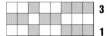 3
1
Colour chart for swatch

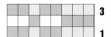 3
1
Colour-variation chart

100

7 ROWS
16 STITCHES

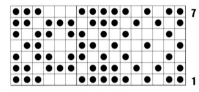 7
1
Black-and-white chart for swatch

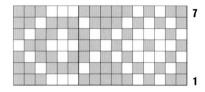 7
1
Colour chart for swatch

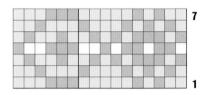 7
1
Colour-variation chart

101

15 ROWS
16 STITCHES

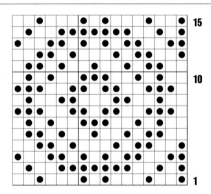 15
10
1
Black-and-white chart for swatch

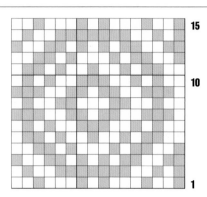 15
10
1
Colour chart for swatch

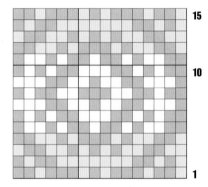 15
10
1
Colour-variation chart

102

5 ROWS
8 STITCHES

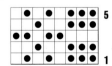 5
1
Black-and-white chart
for swatch

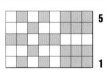 5
1
Colour chart for swatch

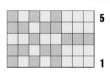 5
1
Colour-variation chart

103

21 ROWS
24 STITCHES

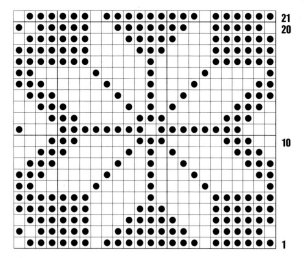

Black-and-white chart for swatch

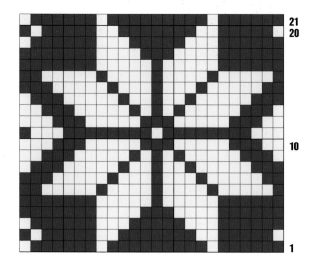

Colour chart for swatch

104

10 ROWS
4 STITCHES

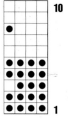

Black-and-white
chart for swatch

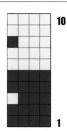

Colour chart
for swatch

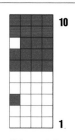

Colour-variation
chart

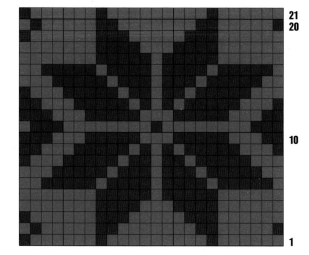

Colour-variation chart

105

6 ROWS
6 STITCHES

Black-and-white
chart for swatch

Colour chart
for swatch

Colour-variation
chart

106

10 ROWS
14 STITCHES

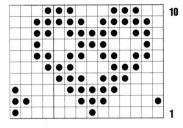

Black-and-white chart for swatch

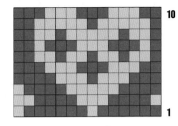

Colour chart for swatch

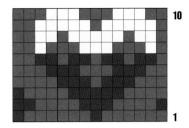

Colour-variation chart

107

15 ROWS
22 STITCHES

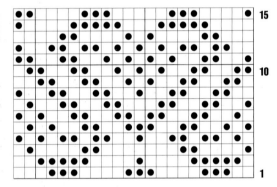

Black-and-white chart for swatch

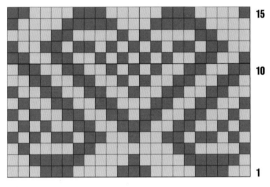

Colour chart for swatch

Colour-variation chart

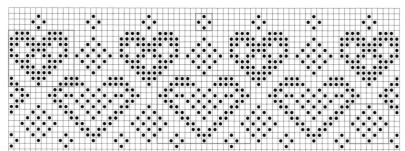

Mix and match motifs 12 + 106 + 162 + 107

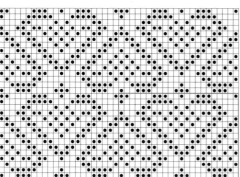

Allover repeat chart

108

9 ROWS
12 STITCHES

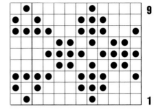

Black-and-white chart for swatch

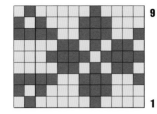

Colour chart for swatch

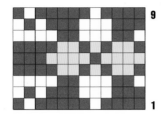

Colour-variation chart

109

19 ROWS
22 STITCHES

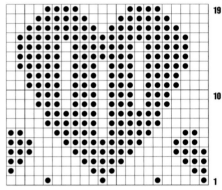

Black-and-white chart for swatch

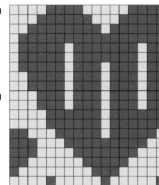

Colour chart for swatch

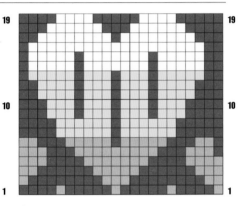

Colour-variation chart

110

13 ROWS
4 STITCHES

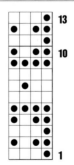

Black-and-white
chart for swatch

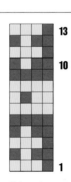

Colour chart
for swatch

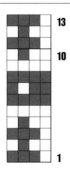

Colour-variation
chart

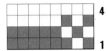

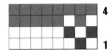

4 ROWS
8 STITCHES

Black-and-white chart for swatch

Colour chart for swatch

Colour-variation chart

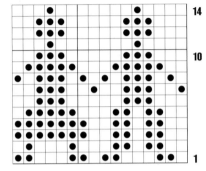

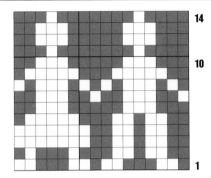

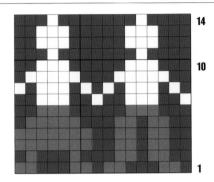

14 ROWS
16 STITCHES

Black-and-white chart for swatch

Colour chart for swatch

Colour-variation chart

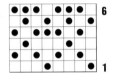

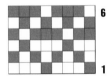

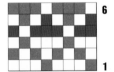

6 ROWS
8 STITCHES

Black-and-white chart for swatch

Colour chart for swatch

Colour-variation chart

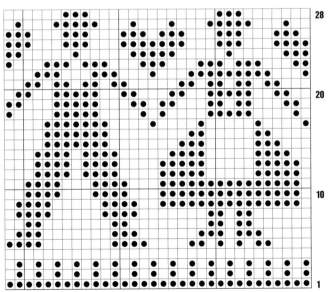

28 ROWS
32 STITCHES

Black-and-white chart for swatch

Colour chart for swatch

115

12 ROWS
12 STITCHES

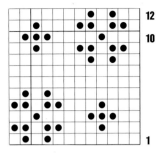

Black-and-white chart for swatch

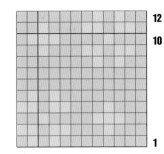

Colour chart for swatch

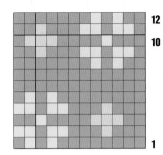

Colour-variation chart

116

16 ROWS
12 STITCHES

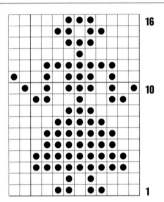

Black-and-white chart for swatch

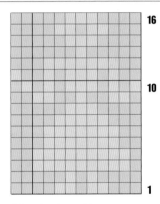

Colour chart for swatch

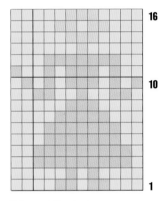

Colour-variation chart

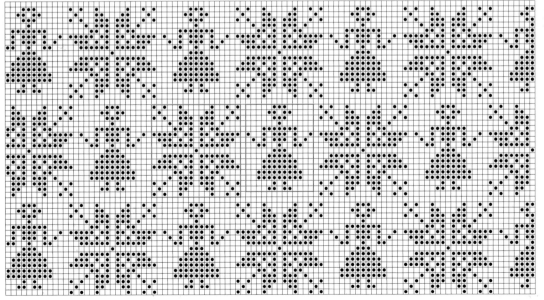

Mix and match motifs
40 + 116 + 98

114

117

7 ROWS
14 STITCHES

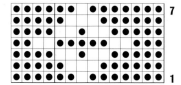

Black-and-white chart for swatch

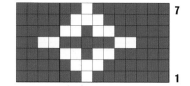

Colour chart for swatch

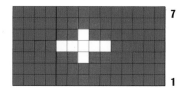

Colour-variation chart

118

4 ROWS
7 STITCHES

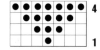

Black-and-white chart for swatch

Colour chart for swatch

Colour-variation chart

119

33 ROWS
14 STITCHES

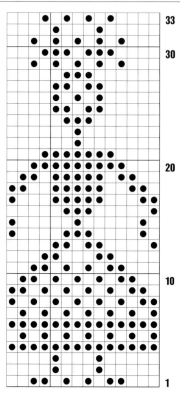

Black-and-white chart for swatch

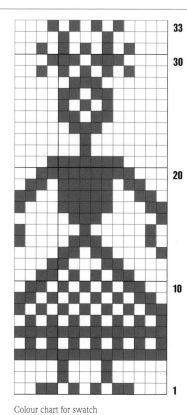

Colour chart for swatch

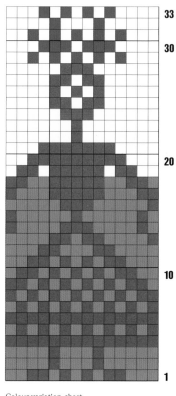

Colour-variation chart

120

5 ROWS
7 STITCHES

Black-and-white chart for swatch

Colour chart for swatch

Colour-variation chart

121

11 ROWS
16 STITCHES

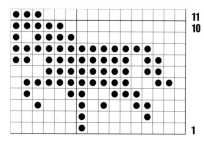

Black-and-white chart for swatch

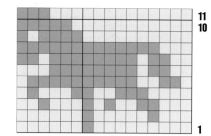

Colour chart for swatch

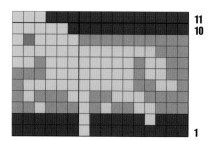

Colour-variation chart

122

2 ROWS
6 STITCHES

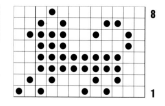

Black-and-white chart for swatch

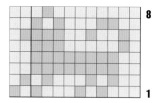

Colour chart for swatch

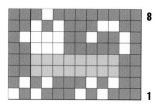

Colour-variation chart

123

17 ROWS
17 STITCHES

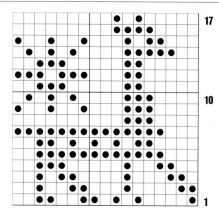

Black-and-white chart for swatch

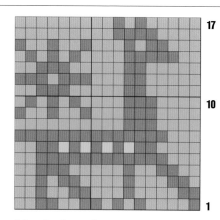

Colour chart for swatch

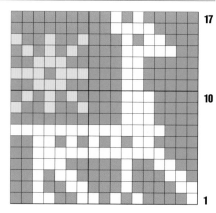

Colour-variation chart

124

3 ROWS
4 STITCHES

Black-and-white chart for swatch

Colour chart for swatch

Colour-variation chart

125

8 ROWS
12 STITCHES

Black-and-white chart for swatch

Colour chart for swatch

Colour-variation chart

126

12 ROWS
18 STITCHES

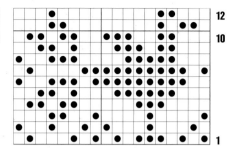

Black-and-white chart for swatch

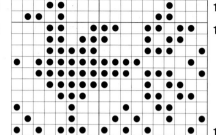

Black-and-white chart for swatch

Colour chart for swatch

127

14 ROWS
6 STITCHES

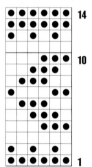

Black-and-white
chart for swatch

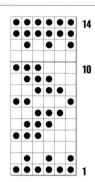

Black-and-white
chart for swatch

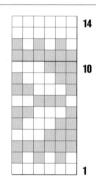

Colour chart for swatch

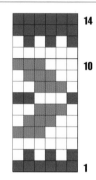

Colour-variation chart

128

18 ROWS
12 STITCHES

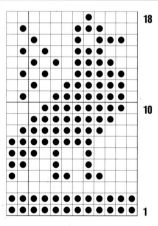

Black-and-white chart for swatch

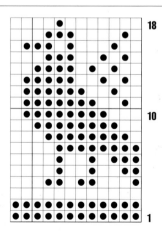

Black-and-white chart for swatch

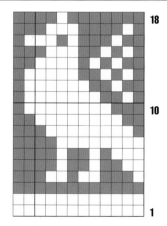

Colour chart for swatch

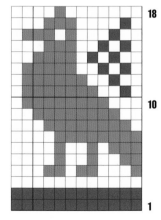

Colour-variation chart

129

8 ROWS
12 STITCHES

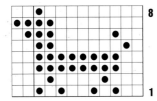

Black-and-white chart for swatch

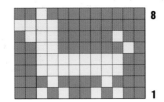

Colour chart for swatch

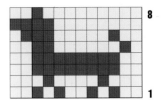

Colour-variation chart

130

11 ROWS
16 STITCHES

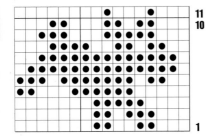

Black-and-white chart for swatch

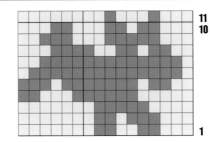

Colour chart for swatch

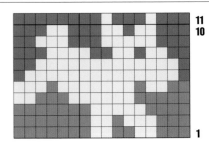

Colour-variation chart

131

4 ROWS
10 STITCHES

Black-and-white chart for swatch

Colour chart for swatch

Colour-variation chart

132

23 ROWS
26 STITCHES

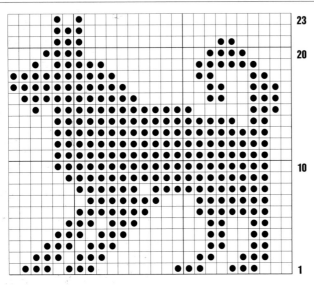

Black-and-white chart for swatch

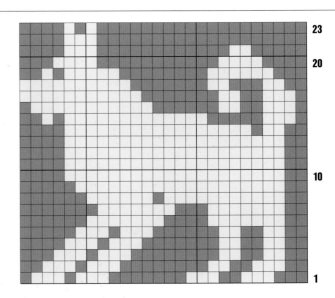

Colour chart for swatch

133

15 ROWS
16 STITCHES

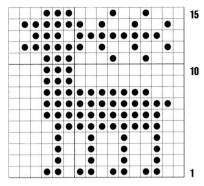

Black-and-white chart for swatch

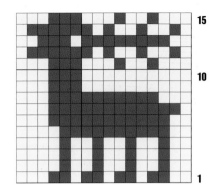

Colour chart for swatch

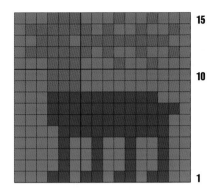

Colour-variation chart

134

5 ROWS
8 STITCHES

Black-and-white chart for swatch

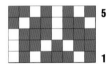

Colour chart for swatch

Colour-variation chart

135

22 ROWS
22 STITCHES

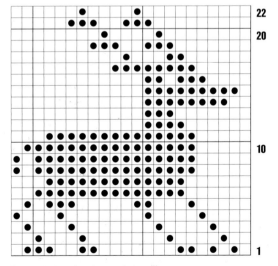

Black-and-white chart for swatch

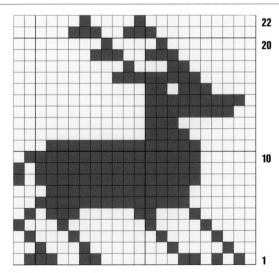

Colour chart for swatch

136

19 ROWS
21 STITCHES

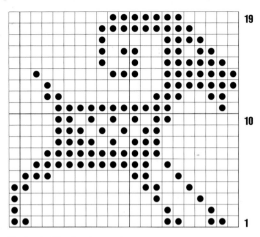

Black-and-white chart for swatch

Colour chart for swatch

137

3 ROWS
6 STITCHES

Black-and-white chart for swatch

Colour chart for swatch

Colour-variation chart

138

20 ROWS
23 STITCHES

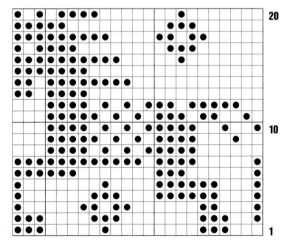

Black-and-white chart for swatch

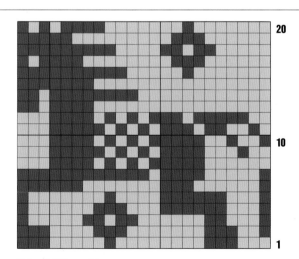

Colour chart for swatch

139

23 ROWS
30 STITCHES

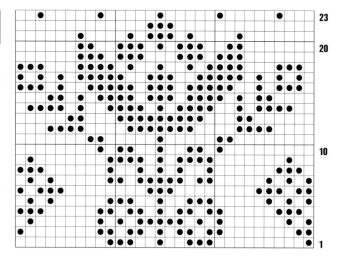

Black-and-white chart for swatch

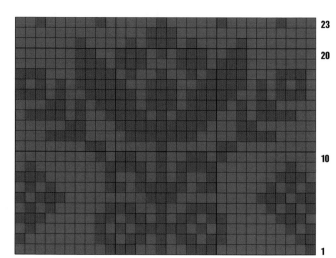

Colour chart for swatch

140

20 ROWS
55 STITCHES

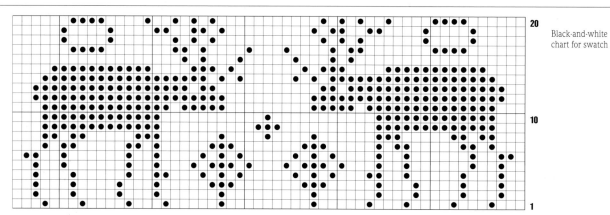

Black-and-white
chart for swatch

Colour chart
for swatch

141

5 ROWS
5 STITCHES

Black-and-white chart for swatch

Colour chart for swatch

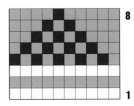

Colour-variation chart

142

8 ROWS
10 STITCHES

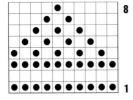

Black-and-white chart for swatch

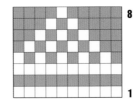

Colour chart for swatch

Colour-variation chart

143

8 ROWS
10 STITCHES

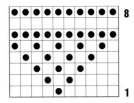

Black-and-white chart for swatch

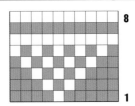

Colour chart for swatch

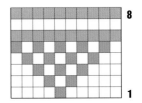

Colour-variation chart

144

26 ROWS
23 STITCHES

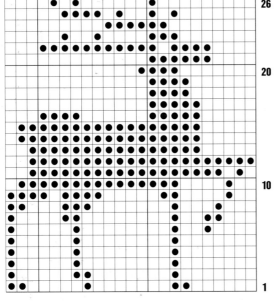

Black-and-white chart for swatch

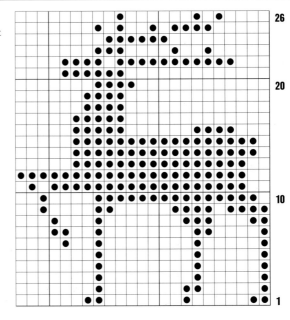

Black-and-white chart for swatch

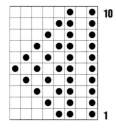

145

10 ROWS
8 STITCHES

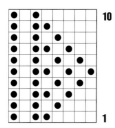

Black-and-white chart
for swatch

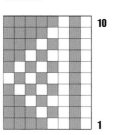

Black-and-white chart
for swatch

Colour chart for swatch

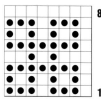

146

8 ROWS
8 STITCHES

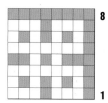

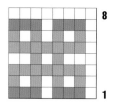

Black-and-white chart for swatch   Colour chart for swatch   Colour-variation chart

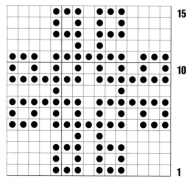

147

15 ROWS
15 STITCHES

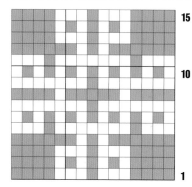

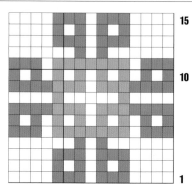

Black-and-white chart for swatch   Colour chart for swatch   Colour-variation chart

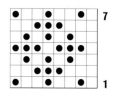

148

7 ROWS
8 STITCHES

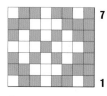

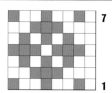

Black-and-white chart for swatch   Colour chart for swatch   Colour-variation chart

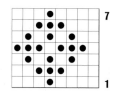

149

7 ROWS
8 STITCHES

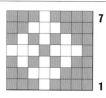

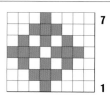

Black-and-white chart for swatch   Colour chart for swatch   Colour-variation chart

150

15 ROWS
15 STITCHES

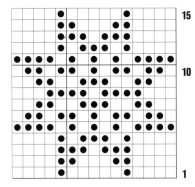

Black-and-white chart for swatch

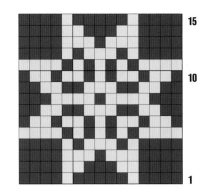

Colour chart for swatch

151

15 ROWS
15 STITCHES

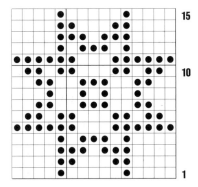

Black-and-white chart for swatch

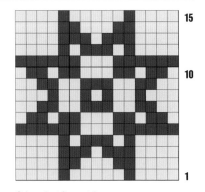

Colour chart for swatch

152

15 ROWS
15 STITCHES

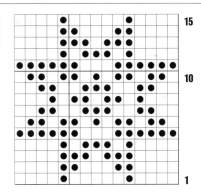

Black-and-white chart for swatch

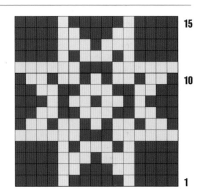

Colour chart for swatch

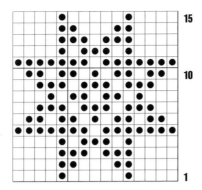

Black-and-white chart for swatch

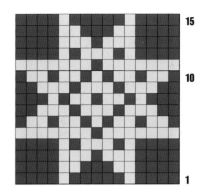

Colour chart for swatch

15 ROWS
15 STITCHES

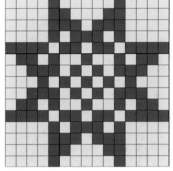

Black-and-white chart for swatch

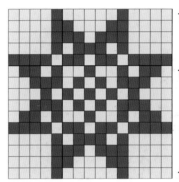

Colour chart for swatch

15 ROWS
15 STITCHES

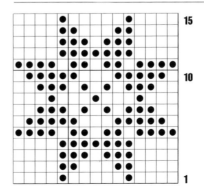

Black-and-white chart for swatch

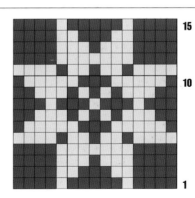

Colour chart for swatch

15 ROWS
15 STITCHES

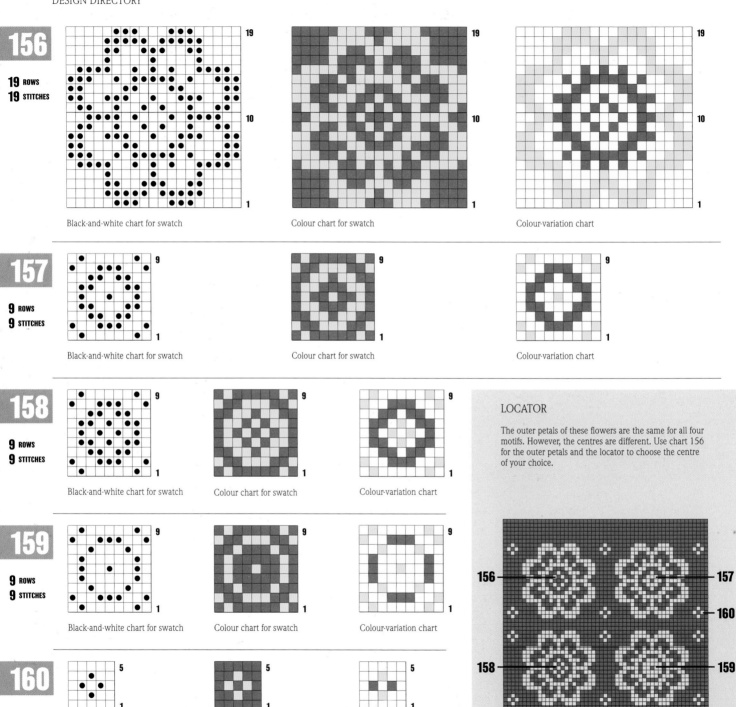

156

19 ROWS
19 STITCHES

Black-and-white chart for swatch

Colour chart for swatch

Colour-variation chart

157

9 ROWS
9 STITCHES

Black-and-white chart for swatch

Colour chart for swatch

Colour-variation chart

158

9 ROWS
9 STITCHES

Black-and-white chart for swatch

Colour chart for swatch

Colour-variation chart

159

9 ROWS
9 STITCHES

Black-and-white chart for swatch

Colour chart for swatch

Colour-variation chart

160

5 ROWS
5 STITCHES

Black-and-white chart for swatch

Colour chart for swatch

Colour-variation chart

LOCATOR

The outer petals of these flowers are the same for all four motifs. However, the centres are different. Use chart 156 for the outer petals and the locator to choose the centre of your choice.

156 — 157

160

158 — 159

161

10 ROWS
30 STITCHES

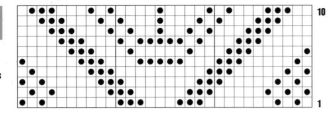

Black-and-white chart for swatch

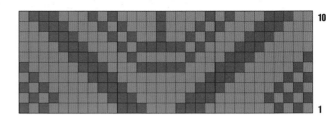

Colour chart for swatch

162

13 ROWS
30 STITCHES

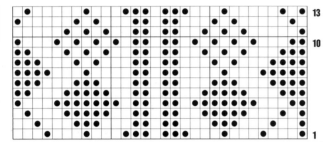

Black-and-white chart for swatch

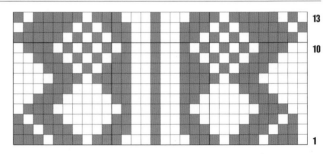

Colour chart for swatch

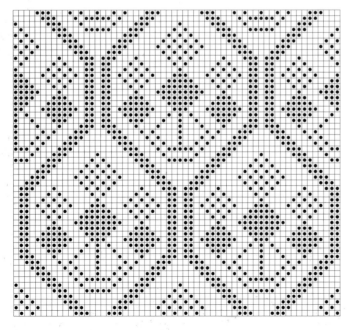

Allover repeat of
motifs 161 + 162

163

24 ROWS
24 STITCHES

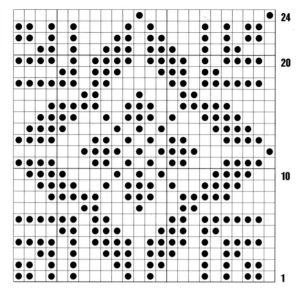

Black-and-white chart for swatch

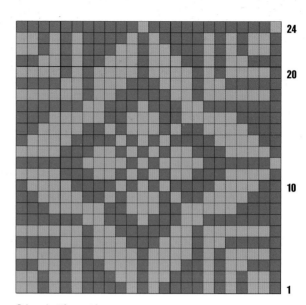

Colour chart for swatch

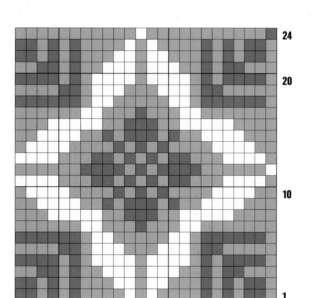

Colour-variation chart

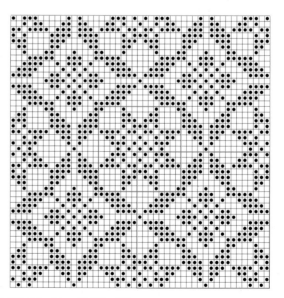

Mix and match motifs 154 + 163

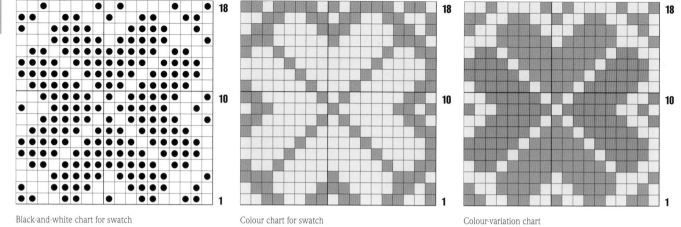

164

18 ROWS
18 STITCHES

Black-and-white chart for swatch

Colour chart for swatch

Colour-variation chart

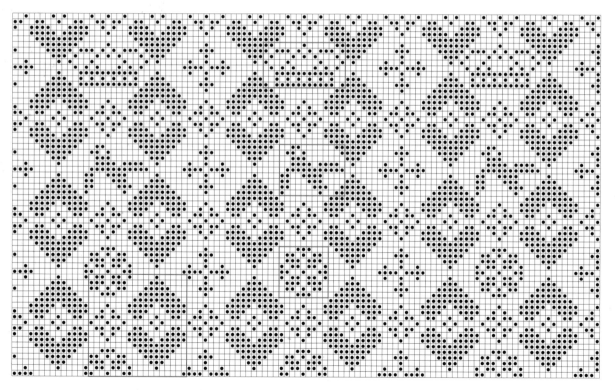

Mix and match motifs 164 + 36 + 73 + 79

165

34 ROWS
34 STITCHES

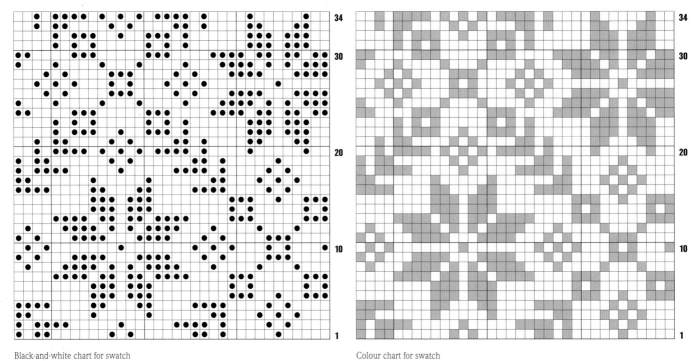

Black-and-white chart for swatch

Colour chart for swatch

Colour-variation chart

Mix and match motifs 165 + 41 + 64

166

26 ROWS
42 STITCHES

167

9 ROWS
19 STITCHES

168

7 ROWS
6 STITCHES

Black-and-white chart for swatch

PROJECTS

The designs in this book can be combined and used in a myriad of ways. This chapter presents a selection of attractive projects, with full making instructions, to inspire you with ideas of how to use them in your own designs.

BLOSSOM PINCUSHION

Try your hand at a tight tension close to that used on many traditional garments with this pincushion. It uses design 159 (page 136) and some strategically placed lice stitches that assure your floats are never too long.

With colour A cast on 46 sts. Place 23 sts on one needle, divide the rem sts onto two needles and join without twisting for working in the round. Work following 27 rnds of chart.

Finishing Combine last 23 sts onto one needle. Turn work inside out. With colour A work 3-needle cast-off. Turn right side out, pulling all loose ends to inside. Wet or steam block flat, carefully folding along colour change. When dry, stuff firmly with wool roving. With tapestry needle and length of colour A, stitch the cast-on edge together using mattress stitch. If needed, poke through the knitted piece with a blunt tapestry needle, or double-pointed needle to arrange the roving so the cushion is pleasing and plump.

MATERIALS

Yarn
100% Norwegian wool (Rauma, 3tr. Strikkegarn), 50g ball = 164m (150yd)
• 1 ball colour A, blue (33/66 Teal)
• 1 ball colour B, grey (103 Gray)

Needles
• 1 set 3.25mm (size 3) double-pointed needles

Notions
• tapestry needle
• wool roving

Tension
23 sts and 27 rnds = 10cm (4in) in colourwork pattern

Finished size
10cm (4in) square

Each side of the pincushion is the reverse colourway of the other, making it a great project to practice colour combinations and help you to determine which colour you prefer for the pattern colour and the background colour.

■ A
□ B

TRADITIONAL MITTENS

Charming mittens reminiscent of the traditional mittens of Gotland, an island off the south eastern coast of Sweden. Featuring a small, easy-to-memorize, three-colour, geometric pattern (a variation of design 10, page 52) and a simple peasant thumb. Only every fourth round uses all three colours, making it a great first project for using more than two colours. You may duplicate stitch the third colour if desired.

MATERIALS

Yarn
100% Norwegian wool (Dale of Norway, Heilo), 50g ball = 100m (109yd)
• 1 ball colour A, red (4018 Red)
• 1 ball colour B, white (0020 Natural)
• 1 ball colour C, grey (0083 Charcoal)

Needles
• set of 3.5mm (size 4) double-pointed needles
• set of 3.75mm (size 5) double-pointed needles

Notions
• tapestry needle
• 2 stitch holders

Tension
25 sts and 27 rnds = (10cm) 4in in colourwork pattern on larger needle

Finished size
Hand circumference 23cm (9¼in), length 23cm (9¼in)

Make two.
With smaller needles and colour A cast on 48 sts. Place 24 sts on one needle, divide the rem sts onto two needles and join without twisting. Work in k1, p1 rib for 5cm (2in).
Increase rnd: * Rib 5 sts, M1; rep from * 9 more times; end p1, k1, p1, M1 – 58 sts. Change to larger needles. Work rnds 1–8 of Chart A two times.
Thumb placement right mitten
Next rnd: K1, place foll 8 sts on stitch holder, with backward loop method, loosely cast 8 sts onto RH needle, work to end of row.

Thumb placement left mitten
Next rnd: (Rnd 1) K 20, place foll 8 sts on stitch holder, with backward loop method, loosely cast 8 sts onto RH needle, work to end of row. Work rnds 2–8 of Chart A. Work Chart A one more time.
Mitten top Work Chart B – 10 sts rem. Combine last 5 sts onto one needle. Turn work inside out and with colour A work 3-needle cast-off. Turn right side out.
Thumb Place 8 sts from stitch holder onto a double-pointed needle with colour A and another needle knit across these 8 sts, with

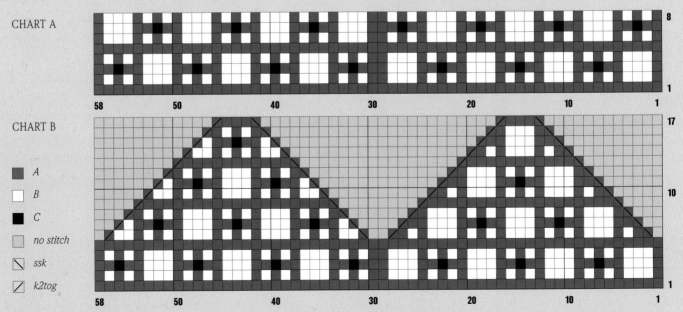

CHART A

CHART B

■ A
□ B
■ C
▦ no stitch
◥ ssk
◤ k2tog

another needle pick up 1 st at the corner of the
opening, and 4 sts above opening, with a third
needle pick up 4 more sts from above opening
and 1 st in the corner of the opening – 18 sts.
Join for working in the round. Work thumb
chart. Break yarn. Thread tail through rem 6 sts
and securely fasten off.

Finishing With tapestry needle weave in ends.
Take special care at points where thumb joins
the body of the mitt. Duplicate stitch thumb in
colour C to match body of the mitten if desired.
Wet block mittens.

LEFT THUMB

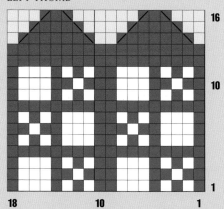

RIGHT THUMB

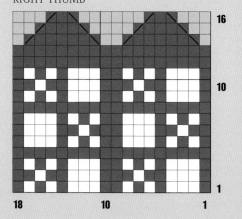

REINDEER HAT

Reindeer (design 67, page 86) march around this retro-inspired hat while snowflakes (made from elements of design 126, page 120) sprinkle from above. A great project to practice a challenging non-symmetrical pattern design, the only shaping occurs when the colourwork is finished.

With smaller needle and colour A cast on 110 sts, place marker and join without twisting. Work k1, p1 rib for 4cm (1½in).
Increase rnd: *Rib 11 sts, M1; repeat from * 9 more times – 120 sts.
Change to larger needle.
Work rnds 1–22 of chart A. (Repeat 15 sts of chart 8 times.)
Decrease rnd: With colour B, *k13, k2tog; rep from * – 112 sts.
Work rnds 1–11 of chart B. (Repeat 14 sts of chart 8 times.)

Crown Shaping
Work in colour B.
Rnd 1: Knit.
Rnd 2: *K5, k2tog; repeat from * 15 more times – 96 sts.
Rnds 3–5: Knit.
Rnd 6: *K4, k2tog; repeat from * 15 more times – 80 sts.
Rnds 7–8: Knit.
Rnd 9: *K3, k2tog; repeat from * 15 more times – 64 sts.
Rnds 10–11: Knit.
Rnd 12: *K2, k2tog; repeat from * 15 more times – 48 sts.
Rnd 13: Knit.
Rnd 14: *K1, k2tog; repeat from * 15 more times – 32 sts.
Rnd 15: Knit.
Rnd16: *K2tog; repeat from * 15 more times – 16 sts.
Rnd 17: *K2tog; repeat from * 7 more times – 8 sts.
Break yarn. Thread tail through last 8 sts. Securely fasten off.

Finishing With tapestry needle weave in ends. Wet block hat over balloon if desired. With remaining yarn make a 9cm (3½in) pom-pom. Fasten to top of hat.

MATERIALS

Yarn
100% superwash wool (Drops, Karisma), 50g ball = 100m (109yd)
• 1 ball colour A, blue (07 Bright Blue)
• 1 ball colour B, white (01 Natural White)

Needles
• 40cm (16in) 3.25mm (size 3) circular needle
• 40cm (16in) 3.75mm (size 5) circular needle
• set of 3.75mm (size 5) double-pointed needles

Notions
• markers
• tapestry needle
• pom-pom maker (if desired)

Tension
23 sts and 24 rnds = 10cm (4in) in colourwork pattern on larger needle

Finished size
circumference 52cm (26¾in), height 25cm (10in)

CHART A

CHART B

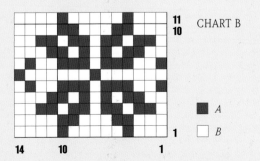

■ A
□ B

GEOMETRIC COWL

A simple cowl with absolutely no shaping is the perfect starting point for your adventures in Scandinavian colourwork. The easy-to-memorize triangle pattern uses the same elements as design 18 (page 59), but offset. Unexpected colour changes further distances this design from the original.

With larger needle and colour A cast on 128 sts. Place marker and join without twisting. Work garter stitch edge as follows:

Rnd 1: Knit.

Rnd 2: Purl.

Repeat rnds 1 and 2 three more times for four garter stitch ridges.

Knit one rnd.

Work rnds 1–8 of chart 5 times.

Work rnds 1–4 once more.

Change to smaller needle and colour A. Work garter stitch edge as follows:

Rnd 1: Knit.

Rnd 2: Purl.

Repeat rnds 1 and 2 three more times. Cast off knitwise. Weave in all ends. Wet block, gently shaping so cast-on edge is slightly wider than cast-off edge.

MATERIALS

Yarn

Aran weight wool (Quince & Co, Lark), 50g ball = 123m (134yd)

- 1 skein colour A, white (1101 Egret)
- 1 skein colour B, green (131 Leek)
- 1 skein colour C, blue (105 Glacier)
- 1 skein colour D, yellow (125 Carrie's Yellow)

Needles

- 40cm (16in) 3.75mm (size 5) circular needle
- 40cm (16in) 4.5mm (size 7) circular needle

Notions

- marker
- tapestry needle

Tension

19 sts and 22 rnds = 10cm (4in) in colourwork pattern on larger needle

Finished size

circumference 66cm (26¼in), height 24cm (9½in)

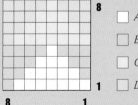

□ A
□ B
□ C
□ D

INDEX

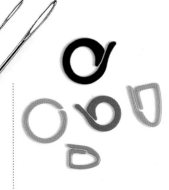

ABBREVIATIONS

foll	follow(ing)
K; k	knit
k2tog	knit 2 together
LH	left hand
M1	make one
P; p	purl
rem	remaining
rep	repeat
RH	right hand
rib	ribbing
rnd	round
st(s)	stitch(es)
ssk	slip slip knit

CREDITS

The author would like to extend special thanks to:

The Nordic Heritage Museum in Seattle,
for generously allowing me to study the hand-knits in
their archive; the Textile Museum of Blönduós, Iceland,
for showing me their amazing collection of knitted shoe
inserts; and my stellar team at Quarto, for their steady
stream of encouragement and thoughtful advice, and
whose gorgeous layouts make everything beautiful.
Thank you!

Quarto would also like to thank the following for
supplying images for inclusion in this book:

32 (t) Arne Ola Grimstad
32 (b) Mona-Lisa Djerf ©Nordiska Museet
33 Garberg Foto, Selbu, Norway,
www.selbuhusflid.no

All other photographs and illustrations are the copyright of
Quarto Publishing plc. While every effort has been made to
credit contributors, Quarto would like to apologize should
there have been any omissions or errors – and would be
pleased to make the appropriate correction for future
editions of the book.

Quarto would like to thank the following for
generously supplying yarn for the book:

Dale of Norway, Heilo
dalegarn.com
Dalekvarm, Norway

Drops, Karisma
garnstudio.com
Oslo, Norway

Quince & Co, Lark
quinceandco.com
Portland, Maine, USA

Rauma, 3tr. Strikkegarn
ramaull.no
Veblugsnes, Norway

Stonehedge Fiber Mill,
Shepherd's Wool
stonehedgefibermill.com
East Jordan, Michigan,
USA

RESOURCES

Christoffersson, Britt-Marie. *Swedish Sweaters: New Designs From Historical Examples*. Newtown, CT: The Taunton Press, 1990.

Flanders, Sue and Kosel, Janine. *Norwegian Handknits: Heirloom Designs from Vesterheim Museum*. Minneapolis, MN: Voyager Press, 2009.

Gibson-Roberts, Pricilla A. and Robson, Deborah. *Knitting in the Old Way: Designs and Techniques from Ethnic Sweaters*. Fort Collins, CO: Nomad Press, 2005.

Gottfridsson, Inger and Ingrid. *The Swedish Mitten Book Traditional Patterns from Gotland*. Asheville, NC: Lark Books, 1984.

Johanson, Britta. *7668 Stjärnor*. Linköping, Sweden: Korsstygnsbolaget, 2009.

Johanson, Britta. *893 Hjärtan Och Kronor*. Linköping, Sweden: Korsstygnsbolaget, 2010.

Jónsdóttir, Védís. *Knitting with Icelandic Wool*. New York, NY: St. Martin's Griffin, 2013.

Keele, Wendy. *Poems of Color: Knitting in the Bohus Tradition*. Loveland, CO: Interweave Press, 1995.

Kulle, Jakob. *Swedish Patterns for Art Weaves and Embroidery*. Stockholm, Sweden: Redivia Publishing House, 2008.

Lind, Vibeke. *Knitting in the Nordic Tradition*. Asheville, NC: Lark Books, 1984.

Ling, Anne-Maj. *Two-End Knitting*. Pittsville, WI: Schoolhouse Press, 2004.

Magnússon, Hélène. *Icelandic Knitting Using Rose Patterns*. Tunbridge Wells, UK: Search Press, 2008.

McGregor, Sheila. *Traditional Scandinavian Knitting*. New York, NY: St. Martin's Press, 1984.

Nargi, Lela. *Knitting Around the World: A Multistranded History of a Time-honored Tradition*. Minneapolis, MN: Voyager Press, 2011.

Norbury, James. *Traditional Knitting Patterns from Scandinavia, the British Isles, France, Italy and other European Countries*. Mineola, NY: Dover Publications, 1974.

Parkes, Clara. *The Knitter's Book of Wool*. New York, NY: Potter Craft, 2009.

Robson, Deborah and Ekarius, Carol. *The Fleece and Fiber Sourcebook: More Than 200 Fibers from Animal to Spun Yarn*. North Adams, MA: Storey Publishing, 2011.

Shea, Terri. *Selbuvotter Biography of a Knitting Tradition*. Seattle, WA: Spinningwheel LLC, 2007.

Sibbern, Annichen. *Norwegian Knitting Designs: Charts and Patterns for Traditional Design*. revised English edition Terri Shea, Spinningwheel LLC, Seattle, WA 2011

Starmore, Alice. *Scandinavian Knitwear: 30 Original Designs from Traditional Patterns*. New York, NY: Van Nostrand Reinhold Company, 1982.

Sundbø, Annemor. *Everyday Knitting: Treasures From a Ragpile*. Kristiansand, Norway: Torridal Tweed, 2001.

Sundbø, Annemor. *Setesdal Sweaters: The History of the Norwegian Lice Pattern*. Kristiansand, Norway: Torridal Tweed, 2001.

Sundbø, Annemor. *Invisible Threads in Knitting*, Kristiansand, Norway: Torridal Tweed, 2007.

150 SCANDINAVIAN
KNITTING DESIGNS

04141547